MODERN
BOAT BUILDING

Revised Edition

EDWIN MONK

MODERN
BOAT BUILDING

CHARLES SCRIBNER'S SONS · New York

This book published simultaneously in the United States of America
and in Canada—Copyright under the Berne Convention

1 3 5 7 9 11 13 15 17 19 M/C 20 18 16 14 12 10 8 6 4 2

Printed in the United States of America
Library of Congress Catalog Card Number: 72-1220
ISBN 0-684-15257-6

CONTENTS

LIST OF FIGURES

PREFACE

THE PROFESSIONAL BOAT BUILDER has the great advantage of having served an apprenticeship, generally two or more years. In Europe in the later part of the last century this was as much as seven years. He started by sweeping the shop and tending the steam box and gradually advanced to journeyman. He benefited by the skills passed down from generations of boat builders.

The amateur or home builder possesses an abundance of enthusiasm and energy but is woefully lacking in information as to how to put his energy efficiently to work. Hopefully this book will, to a worthwhile extent, open for him the breadth of knowledge possessed by the professional craftsman.

The professional may also profit by several tables shown herein, compiled on building costs for both time and material.

The methods shown here are pretty well standard throughout the boat-building world, and if carefully followed they will result in a well-constructed craft that, with proper design, will be seaworthy and weatherly.

The first issue of *Modern Boat Building* appeared in 1939 in the era before waterproof plywood and fiberglass and before the boating world in general had heard of ferro-cement for boat construction.

A few hulls had been built of aluminum, but the modern salt-water alloys were almost unheard of. Today one can build of this material with complete confidence that it will not disintegrate, provided that certain standards of procedures are adhered to.

FIG. 1. There is something about the building of a boat . . .

1/ IN GENERAL

INGRAINED IN MOST OF US IS A CREATIVE SPIRIT, and nowhere can this find a better reward than in building a boat. The realization should and can be a thing of beauty and, as the poet has said, "a joy forever." As with almost all things connected with the sea, there is considerable romance associated with all manner of boats, whether they be cargo carriers, fishermen, or just an average man's pleasure boat. Historians tell us that this has been so all down the ages from the time a man first drifted down a river on a log with a stick in his hands for a paddle. The ancient and the primitive people took great pride in their craft and associated them with all sorts of real and vague personalities, as witness the decorations on the Phoenician and Viking ships and on the war canoes of our own Northwest Indians. Our clipper ships had their beautifully carved figure-heads, and while these have vanished with the passing of the clipper ship, we still endow our boats with names of romance and adventure. We also continue to sacrifice not a little in convenience and practicability to graceful lines and an appearance pleasing to the eye.

Considerable pleasure may be had in constructing a piece of furniture or even a house, but after all it is something inanimate, while to build a boat is to produce a thing of life and character. Few occupations offer an equal outlet for man's inborn urge to build something, and there is neither monotony nor drudgery nor very hard labor; instead there is variety and light clean work, just difficult enough to challenge one's ability and hold one's interest.

One need not build or contemplate building to be interested in the boat builder's art. The owner or yachtsman having one constructed, or for that matter already in possession of a boat, is naturally interested in construction methods and standard practice. He is, however, at a disadvantage in not having technical knowledge or experience to guide him as to how things should be done, and information regarding this subject is not readily available.

1

Various factors, one of them the crowding of our highways, have awakened or promoted a revival in boating, and people have come to realize that there is no better form of recreation. More boats are being constructed today than ever before, and more amateurs are building their own boats. Many high schools in coastal cities have boat-building classes in connection with their regular manual-training curriculum, and vocational schools teaching boat building exclusively have also been established. It is for the students in these schools, the apprentice in the boat shop, the amateur building his dream boat at home, and anyone interested in how boats are constructed that this book is proposed as a guide and textbook.

The professional builder can also perhaps glean some useful information, not so much in construction methods but from some of the cost data, rigging, and other details contained herein.

It would be well to state here that the construction of a boat, excepting the simplest of boxlike punts, requires considerable natural mechanical ability or previous experience. As most amateurs who tackle a boat do so partly because they enjoy working with tools, they therefore possess natural ability and from my observation generally wind up with a serviceable boat. Previous experience is of course a wonderful aid. One amateur of my acquaintance built first a "Snipe," which is comparatively easy to build; his next boat was a twenty-one-foot keel sloop and his latest a thirty-four-footer. He has done a job that would be a credit to any boat shop. It is not my purpose to discourage anyone or shake his confidence, but no one should undertake the task with the impression that building a boat is no trick at all.

THE PLANS

The wisdom of building from proper plans by a competent naval architect cannot be too strongly stressed. Not only are time and labor saved, but the builder can be reasonably certain that the boat will meet his expectations, have a trim appearance, and perform as a properly designed boat should perform.

"A little knowledge is a dangerous thing," and nowhere is this phrase better applied than to naval architecture. There are amateur and semi-professional designers scattered throughout the land who for a small fee or none at all will draw up your plans. Perfection in marine design is gained only by years of experience and study; the fee that a recognized naval architect will charge you is the best money you can spend on the boat. I am not stating this with any idea of putting in an oar for my own profession but because personal observation has convinced me that it is true. Your boat will not only be a better boat but it will have a decidedly greater resale value should the time ever come when you wish to dispose of it.

The possibility of wishing to sell the boat at some future time should always

FIG. 2. Basic hull shapes and basic plans

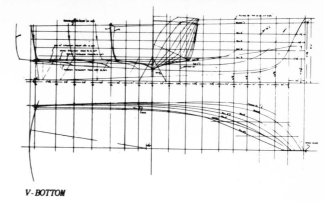

V-BOTTOM

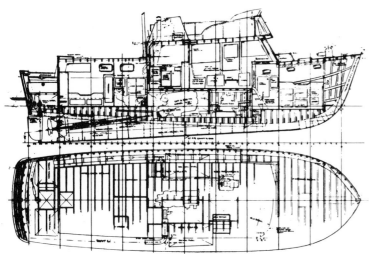

INBOARD PROFILE

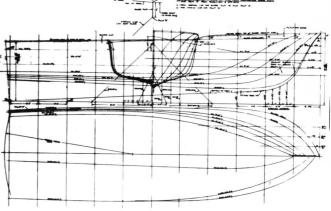

SEMI-PLANING ROUND BOTTOM

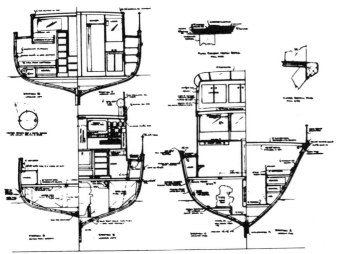

CONSTRUCTION SECTION

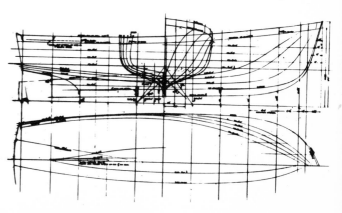

ROUND BOTTOM DISPLACEMENT

be kept in mind. Boat owners are never satisfied, and in a few years you may have something larger or faster in mind. If your present boat can be sold at a favorable figure, a new one will probably be built. There are of course other reasons or possibilities, some of them not too pleasant to contemplate but nevertheless to be reckoned with.

TOOLS

It seems that no matter of what material the hull may be built, some, at least a few, wood-working tools will be needed.

There is some woodwork connected with the making of patterns, forms, etc. for the hull and of course the interior joiner work, and generally the superstructure, bulkheads, floors, and often the decks are wood.

The impression that a large number of expensive and elaborate machine tools are required is erroneous. Fairly large, heavily built schooners have been built with no machine tools at all and the planking ripped out with a sharp hand saw. It pays the boat shop, of course, to be elaborately equipped with labor-saving machinery, but in building one boat only a few pieces are really required.

For a boat of any size, a power band saw is a great help, also an electric hand drill. The combination bench saw, drill press, lathe, etc., turned out for the home workshop will also be found very useful.

Aside from ordinary hand tools in common use, the builder of a wood hull will require a few special hand tools. For planking he will need a hold on. This may consist of a short piece of shafting or maul head and is used to hold against the frame when driving planking nails.

Other tools are a small bevel, as shown in Fig. 3, for planking, also a

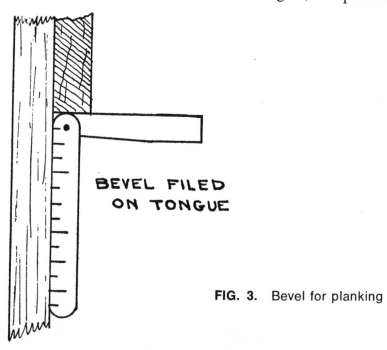

BEVEL FILED
ON TONGUE

FIG. 3. Bevel for planking

larger bevel, a wooden rabbet plane for fairing up planking, and some boat clamps, at least a half dozen. You may have to make the small bevel, using two strips of brass and a rivet.

Wooden planes are seldom available, though universally used for some work by the professional. You will probably have to settle for steel ones. A wood smoothing plane is much superior for smoothing off the hull, and a jack plane or jointer, either iron or wood, is a necessity for fairing up plank edges at the bench.

You will need, of course, a small caulking iron (wood boat), and the hand drill with the turning handle on the side is much superior to the push type. When selecting bitts, avoid the large worm, as it will often split the plank end, and be sure your bitt fits the plugs.

BUILDING COSTS

Building your own boat spreads the construction over quite a long period, thus making it possible to finance it as the work progresses. However, a few hasty figures are likely to prove deceptive. Often the cost of the lumber order is carefully figured under the impression that, aside from the power plant, this will be the major cost. Roughly speaking, it is really about 20 percent of the total. Hardware, tanks, fittings, fastenings, and other items make up the balance, and the cost of all these should be carefully ascertained, with a little more added for items overlooked and unforeseen expenses.

After all, the prime motive in building one's own boat is the saving derived. There are other reasons, generally secondary, however, such as the pride of accomplishment and the natural urge to build. A father may envision a healthy and wholesome employment of his son's spare time and an outlet for his surplus energy. The fact remains, though, that those who can abundantly afford it generally purchase the completed boat ready to step into and start cruising.

The boat builder, amateur or professional, is therefore vitally interested in building costs and the amateur especially in the amount of saving he can realize by doing part or all the work himself. I have constructed the graphs (Fig. 4) to show how the average boat dollar is distributed. Material and labor costs vary greatly with conditions and locality, and it is too much to expect more than a rough estimate from any such chart, no matter how carefully compiled. For instance, one builder could plank his boat with teak, another with pine; one owner may equip his boat lavishly and another very plainly, thus throwing these items out of proportion. All sailors know that whereas the local sailmaker may make a good suit of sails for $500, several firms in the cup-defender class will charge three times this amount.

The item of motor accessories is shown to be more than one-quarter for the power boat and for the sailboat about one-third the cost of the motor. By accessories is meant all items and equipment pertaining to the propelling equipment aside from the motor. As this estimate may seem high, I have listed these items required on a small four-cylinder gas engine of probably about 80 horsepower. With expensive motors, this ratio will be lower, and with the cheaper motor it will not be quite high enough.

The list (Fig. 5) will show the importance of carefully listing each part or item entering into the construction of the boat. Without first obtaining complete plans and specifications, this of course cannot be done; however, an approximate estimate can be made using the cost graphs or charts. They should be useful to the professional builder also as a rough check on his figures and will prevent the wide divergence in bids, so often noted, in which someone always bids too low, to his sorrow.

COST ESTIMATE

The amount of lumber required in the building of the average wood power cruiser is shown by the following curve (Fig. 6). Heavily built boats will run a little over and lightly built ones a little less. The length overall will give the total amount to be used in the construction of the boat, and from this figure we can closely estimate the cost of the lumber.

FIG. 4.

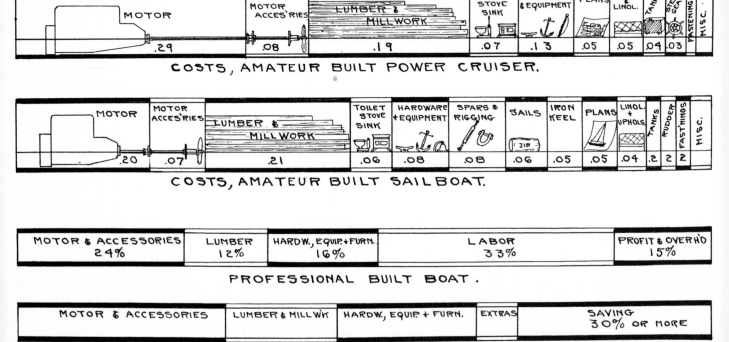

COSTS, AMATEUR BUILT POWER CRUISER.

COSTS, AMATEUR BUILT SAILBOAT.

PROFESSIONAL BUILT BOAT.

COST COMPARISON – AMATEUR BUILT.

FIG. 5. Motor Accessories

Stuffing Box	$ 20.00
Stern Bearing	17.00
Shaft	60.00
Propeller	75.00
Intake Scoop	9.50
Sea Cock	22.00
Silencer and Exhaust Pipe	40.00
Controls	70.00
Copper Tubing	12.00
Fuel Strainer	17.00
Valves	16.50
Starting Cable	12.00
Engine Hold-down Bolts	8.00
Battery	48.00
Machine Work	50.00
Misc.	20.00
Instrument Panel Including Tachometer	65.00
Tachometer Cable	17.00
	$579.00

FIG. 6.

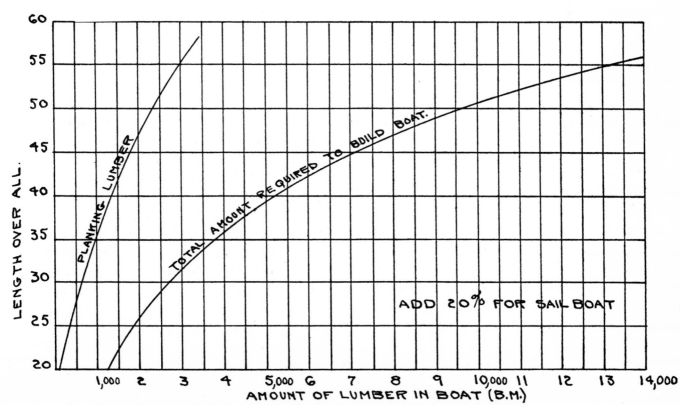

The only way to arrive at an accurate cost of the lumber order is to take the items one by one and price them out.

In arriving at the cost per thousand feet, the lumber is divided roughly into three equal parts or classifications. These are as follows: one—planking and decking; two—framing and bulkheads; by this is meant keel, stem, floors, stringers, deck beams, etc., but not bent oak ribs. The third division is finish lumber and hardwood, hardwood to include frames, hardwood trim, cabin trunks, guards, interior finish lumber, and miscellaneous. There will, of course, be several kinds of hardwood at different prices, but a general average can be roughly estimated.

FIG. 7. Total Cost

As an example we will take the lumber required for a forty-five-foot power cruiser, shown by the chart to be 6,500 feet.

33⅓%	Planking	$350 per M.
33⅓%	Framing and Bulkheads	250 per M.
33⅓%	Hardwood, Interior Finish	600 per M.
		$1,200

$1,200 ÷ 3 = $400 average cost per 1,000 feet, or $2,600 total. The home builder may have to add something for millwork.

Assuming we have the cost of the motor, we can add roughly one-fourth of this for accessories and to this the cost of lumber and plans. Referring to the graph on total cost, we now have for the amateur builder approximately 60 percent of the total. Dividing by 6 and multiplying by 10, we arrive at a cost estimate which, while it may not be exact, is a whole lot better than even an educated guess.

Because the sailboat is more heavily constructed, at least 15 percent should be added to the lumber order. We also have the matter of ballast, sails, rigging, and spars to take into account. The power plant is generally placed with exhaust manifold below the waterline, which requires goosenecks and water-cooled exhaust pipes, thus making a more expensive installation; this is taken care of in the graph. All these things run up the sailing craft's cost 20 to 35 percent above that of a power boat of the same overall length. A smaller outlay is required for the power plant, but a larger one in almost all other directions.

In estimating the cost, the more items we can include, the closer will be the result. The keel casting will be so much a pound; the foundry can tell us what this will be. The sailmaker has a rough method of estimating this item if you can tell him the number of square feet and rig. The lumber order, motor, etc., and all other obtainable items are summed up and the same procedure followed as with the power boat.

COST ESTIMATING BY THE PROFESSIONAL

The professional builder with years of experience should have a wealth of records and cost sheets upon which to base his estimates. Quite often, however, he is a boat builder first and a businessman second. Those of us who are professionally interested in the industry are constantly struck by the wide divergence in bid prices. Sometimes the high bid is twice the lowest. This means, of course, that someone has made a mistake and taken the job at a figure far below his actual costs, let alone a profit.

I would not suggest that the cost data here be used as a basis for figuring or placing a bid, but it should be of real value as a check on the builder's figures. A little judgment and adjusting of this method to the class of boat under consideration will bring fairly close results. Unless extremely efficient, beware of the upper hours curve. When a rough estimate is required by a client, these tables should be particularly useful.

The graph (Fig. 8) shows the amount of steel in the average steel cruiser.

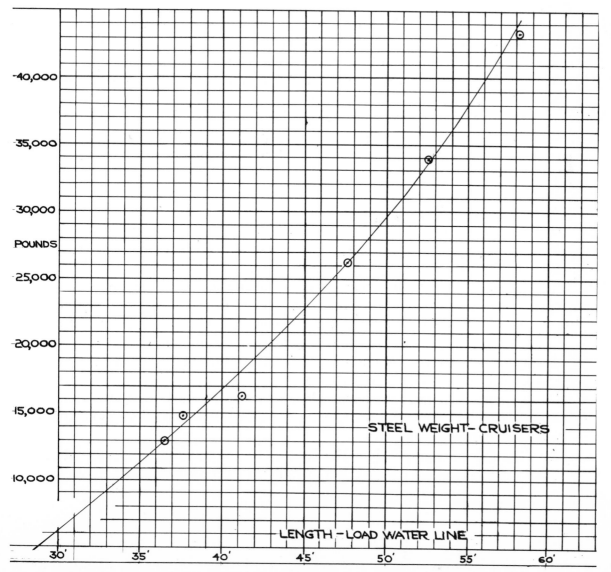

FIG. 8.

As will be mentioned later, one disadvantage of this material, except for heavy-duty ocean cruisers, both sail and power, is its weight. Therefore in this estimate it is contemplated that decks and superstructure will be wood. There would probably be just a steel margin or deck stringer plate around the deck edge and perhaps four steel bulkheads, one at each end of the motor compartment and at the forepeak, and an aft or lazarette bulkhead. Other bulkheads would be wood, as also would be the walking floors. The hull would be of lighter material, which would all add up to a much lighter boat than the work boat.

Another graph (Fig. 9) shows the amount of steel in the average fishing vessel, and this would not be far off if applied to the North Sea trawler type of yacht with steel house. I am indebted to my friend Naval Architect H. C. Hanson for this data.

In estimating the cost of an aluminum boat, the weight of the material itself is about one-third that of steel, but since it possesses less strength, the thickness of plating should be increased by about 30 percent and shapes 50 percent. This means that total weight of material will be about one-half that shown in the graph for steel.

It should be stressed here, however, that all the above is somewhat empirical and that particularly in a steel vessel hull weights can vary by a considerable percentage. One designer, in an attempt at lightness, may corrugate the bottom and dispense with longitudinals; another may stay with the conventional or even heavy it up a bit.

There are rule books covering yacht construction, though none to my knowledge of U.S. origin. Lloyds of London publishes such a book, but designers seem not always to be guided by them, particularly in the smaller and lighter boats.

HOURS OF LABOR

Here again is an important item to both amateur and professional and indeed very vital to the latter.

The factor of efficiency enters into this to such an extent that an inefficient operation may employ twice the hours of an efficient one.

An efficiently laid-out shop will, of course, make a difference, but the largest factor is experience, along with, perhaps, the *esprit de corps*. A shop that does new work entirely, with no repair or haul-out facilities, is the most efficient and seems to attract the better workmen.

I suppose the amateur should add a sizable percentage for broken hours, inexperience, and less sophisticated equipment, though he may compensate somewhat in energy and enthusiasm.

The following graph (Fig. 10) is based on information furnished by boat shops for one-at-a-time building, not quantity production. One should, however,

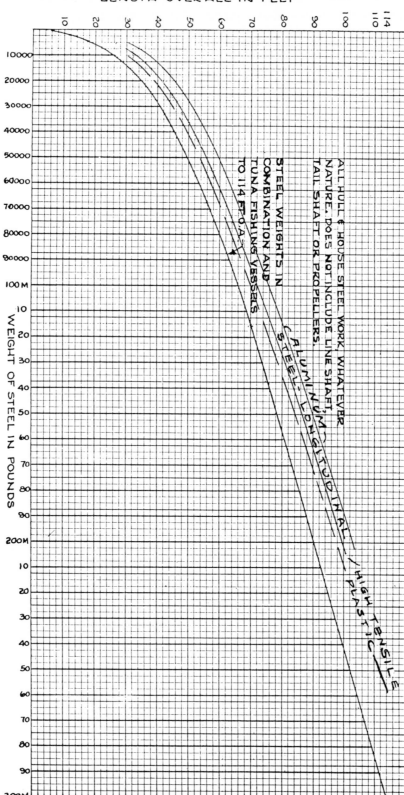

LENGTH OVER ALL IN FEET

WEIGHT OF STEEL IN POUNDS

ALL HULL & HOUSE STEEL WORK WHATEVER
NATURE. DOES NOT INCLUDE LINE SHAFT,
TAIL SHAFT OR PROPELLERS.

STEEL WEIGHTS IN
COMBINATION AND
TUNA FISHING VESSELS
TO 114 FT. O.A.

ALUMINUM

STEEL - LONGITUDINAL

HIGH TENSILE

PLASTIC

FIG. 9.

not be deceived by the top curve, as this was based on an extremely efficient operation by workmen who built boat after boat. A combination repair and construction shop may easily require almost double this amount of time and some amateurs an unbelievable amount. One case had 11,000 hours on a forty-two-foot cruiser.

Hours of labor on a metal boat, when the finished product is considered, should not vary greatly from the above and in some instances might even be a little less. The steel boat should be sandblasted or treated plates used, but sandblasting is usually a hired operation.

The fiberglass hull, unless a mold is available, would consume considerably more time, as the "plug," as it is termed, involves perhaps two-thirds the labor of building a wooden hull, and polishing the mold itself is a painstaking operation. More on this in Chapter 16.

Ferro-cement also is high in labor cost though very economical otherwise, and this is its appeal to the home builder.

FIG. 10.

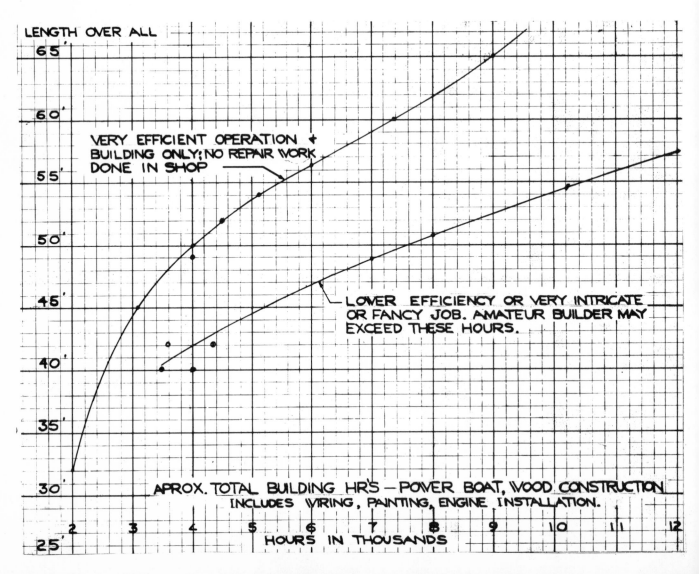

2/ BOAT-BUILDING MATERIALS

THE CHOICE OF MATERIALS for the wood boat is largely governed by the locality in which it is being built. Some woods commonly used and readily available in one locality may be unheard of or hard to obtain in others. Oak is always used for bent frames and generally for the sawed frames of V-bottom boats, and it is practically the only wood universally available. Some species of cedar or cypress, almost any one of which is ideal for planking, is generally obtainable.

Longitudinal strength members such as stringers, clamps, and keel requiring long length are chiefly of some species of pine. Douglas fir is ideal for this purpose.

Decks, where caulked, require a wood with a minimum of shrinkage, teak being without a peer for the purpose. Vertical grain Douglas fir, white, and some of the other pines, as well as the harder cedars and mahogany, are also commonly used.

For exterior trim, and in fact almost anywhere throughout the boat, teak is without doubt the finest boat-building material. There is a saying that no one has ever seen a rotten piece of teak, and boats well over two hundred years old bear this out. It contains an oil that seems to prevent moisture from entering and can go unvarnished and neglected for long periods with little blemish when refinished, whereas mahogany stains and blackens under similar conditions.

Weight being quite a factor in light fast hulls, a table (Fig. 11) showing the weights per cubic foot of various woods is given for reference.

THE HULL STRUCTURE

A hull should be considered more or less as a truss with the keel and bottom planking forming the lower member, and the deck, clamp and sheer and upper

13

FIG. 11

SPECIES	POUNDS, Dry	POUNDS, Wet
Ash	40	49
Birch	32	57
Butternut	35	45
Cedar, Western red	24	41
Cedar, Oregon or Port Orford	31	39
Cedar, white	22	41
Cedar, Spanish	35	42
Cedar, Alaska	31	39
Cypress	31	—
Elm	45	48
Douglas fir or Oregon pine	32	40
Hackmatack	35	—
Hickory	48	—
Locust	46	66
Honduras mahogany	44	50
Philippine mahogany	39	—
Maple	43	46
Oak, white	46	62
White pine	26	39
Oregon pine	32	40
Yellow pine	44	47
Spruce	27	38
Teak	48	58

strakes the top. Planking and framing in between are more or less neutral but act as bracing between the two halves of the truss.

It should be mentioned that there are several species of wood sold under the name of Philippine mahogany, and they vary greatly in weight and hardness. The hard red Philippine is used largely for planking and is, as the name implies, very hard and also heavy. A lighter species called Luan is both lighter in weight and color and not as hard or as strong.

DURABILITY

Opposite (Fig. 12) is listed the durability of various boat-building woods as obtained from data by U.S. Forest Products Laboratory.

SPECIES	ABILITY TO STAY IN PLACE	WORKABILITY	NAIL HOLDING ABILITY	EASE WITH WHICH WOODS CAN BE GLUED	DURABILITY BASED ON THAT OF WHITE OAK AS 100 PER CENT
SOFTWOODS					
CEDAR, ALASKA + PORT ORF.	II	I	IV	II	125-175
CEDAR, WESTERN RED	II	I	IV	II	125-175
CEDAR, WHITE	II	I	IV	II	80-100
CYPRESS, BALD	II	II	IV	II	125-175
DOUGLAS FIR	II	II	III	I	75-100
HEMLOCK, WESTERN	II	II	III	I	35-55
PINE, PITCH		III	III	II	45-55
PINE, SOUTHERN YELLOW	II	II	III	I	40-100
PINE, WESTERN WHITE	II	I	IV	I	65-80
REDWOOD	II	I	IV	I	125-175
SPRUCE, SITKA	II	II	IV	I	35-50
TAMARACK		III	III	II	75-85
HARDWOODS					
ALDER, RED		I		I	
ASH, WHITE	I	I	I	III	40-55
BIRCH, PAPER	II	I	II	V	35-50
BUTTERNUT	I	I	IV	II	50-70
ELM, WHITE	II	III	II	I	50-70
HICKORY SHAGBARK	II	III	I	IV	40-55
LOCUST, HONEY	I	III	I	V	80-100
MAPLE, OREGON		III	IV	V	40-50
OAK, RED	III	II	I	III	40-55
OAK, WHITE	II	II	I	I	100
MAHOGANY HONDURAS	I	II	II	I	100
TEAK	I	I	II	III	INFINITE

FIG. 12.

In some parts of the boat, such as interior joiner work, where it is assumed that there will be adequate ventilation, finish rather than durability is of great importance. For planking, framing, beams, stem, etc., a rot-resistant wood is most important.

GALVANIC ACTION

When two dissimilar metals are immersed in salt water there is set up an electrical current between the two, and one of the metals gradually wastes away. This is termed electrolysis and is in some instances a very serious problem. Thin-hulled metal lifeboats converted to cruisers have been so pitted by this action as to be rendered totally useless.

The wasted metal is termed the less noble and the other one the noble metal. The following scale is termed the galvanic series. Submerged metals should not be too far apart in this series. As an example, if you have a monel shaft and a galvanized rudder, the galvanizing will soon disappear. You should not, even inside the boat, directly connect a copper tube to an aluminum tank. On the other hand, certain alloys of stainless-steel shafts are used in steel and aluminum hulls, as they are not far apart in the series.

In sailboats cast-iron keels are quite compatible with manganese bronze rudder fittings. They are close together in the galvanic scale (Fig. 13).

FIG. 13. GALVANIC SERIES

Most Noble, Electro-Negative, or Protected Metal
↓
Mercury and Mercury Paint
Monel
Nickel
Silicon Bronze (Everdure: one trade name)
Copper and Copper Paint
Red Brass
Aluminum Bronze
Gun Metal and Admiralty Brass
Yellow Brass
Phosphor Bronze
Manganese Bronze
Lead
Stainless Steel, Active (most stainless-steel fittings)
Cast Iron
Wrought Iron
Mild Steel
Aluminum
Cadmium
Galvanized Iron and Steel
Zinc
Magnesium
↑
Least Noble

KEEL

The keel is, of course, the backbone of the structure to which ribs are fastened. Contrary to popular opinion, however, it does not in itself lend greatly to the fore and aft strength of the boat, except that it acts as one of the bottom members of a truss alternately in tension and compression, and for this reason should if possible be in one length. The shoe is merely a protection for the keel, mainly against teredos and marine borers which will enter wherever the copper paint is knocked off.

For keels one should avoid the heart of the tree, as when the timber dries it may take a very serious twist. This is one reason laminated sticks are excellent.

FLOORS

Floors are important in that they tie the heels of the frames together and give the boat considerable thwartship stiffness and help to counteract ringing stress.

Floors should be well fastened to keel as well as to frames. Some designs call for floors alongside frames and others on top. As a deeper floor is possible with the former method and as the floor also forms a bearing fastening for planking, I believe this is the best practice.

FRAMES

Frames are almost always of bent white oak, except in sawed frame and V-bottom construction. A weak or poorly constructed frame cannot be strengthened after the boat is built. Keel, planking, or almost any other part of the boat can be, but very seldom the frame. Therefore, care should be exercised in seeing that the ribs of the structure are of ample size and that they are properly bent, or, if sawed, well fastened together.

PLANKING

Planking is of course the hull of the boat, frames, beams, stringers, and other members being auxiliary to it. It provides the major fore and aft strength and for this reason should be in long lengths with butts or joints well spaced. Short lengths and butts are not objectionable at the ends where little if any bending stresses occur. Double planking with one or more layers diagonal is the strongest type of hull, and as the diagonal planking also serves as framing, the size of the latter can be reduced.

When a boat is built in a rather damp climate such as the Pacific Northwest and may cruise in warm Southern waters, the topsides should be double planked right down to the waterline, forward in particular.

Several boats have come near to sinking when these seams opened up and the bow wave literally poured in.

SHELVES AND CLAMPS

Shelves and clamps perform two functions, the chief of which is to tie the deck to the sides and next to provide fore and aft strength. They should be heavy enough to hold fastenings properly and not too cross-grained.

BILGE STRINGERS

Bilge stringers distribute the effect of a blow or pressure over several frames and distribute the transverse strength imparted to a hull by bulkheads, and like clamps and shelves they should be in long lengths or fitted with long scarfs. One strake should be so placed that in heeling over when aground it will be at or near the point of contact or bearing.

BULKHEADS

Bulkheads add immeasurably to the strength of a hull. A large steel boat obtains most of its thwartship strength and resistance to racking stress from them. They should be well secured to frames and beams, fit tightly against them, and, if of fairly large area, stiffened against buckling.

THE DECK

As well as closing off the top of the boat from wind and water, the deck imparts to the boat its greatest resistance against horizontal racking. Especially is this true with sailboats. For this reason a diagonal layer is sometimes laid first or lodging knees installed. A well-fastened plywood deck accomplishes the same end.

In any case, whether for power or sail, the decking should be well secured to the beams and tightly fitted. The caulking in a caulked deck wedges the pieces tightly together and helps greatly to resist racking. A weak canvased tongue and groove deck of a sailboat will often wrinkle alternately one way and then the other as the boat changes tacks. Canvas is, however, seldom used today.

CEILING

Ceiling, where heavy or continuous, imparts strength to the structure, but the tendency in late years has been either to dispense with it altogether or to limit its use to a narrow strip at the bilge. This has been a decided improvement. Frames and planking are thus more accessible for inspection, and the chances of dry rot are greatly reduced. To compensate for the lack of ceiling, planking is made a little heavier or the boat may be double planked; bilge stringers and other interior members are also increased in size.

STEM

Hardness and resistance to dry rot and damage in case of collision are desirable in stem material. It should of course be of some wood that will not check or split easily and that will hold fastenings well.

CAULKING

Caulking not only makes the hull watertight but, as it wedges each plank tightly against its neighbor, stiffens the hull immeasurably. The old wooden ship was heavily ceiled, and each strake of ceiling was heavily wedged against the next with wooden wedges driven in with a wooden maul or beadle. When an old boat showed signs of weakness or hogging, it was sometimes rewedged and recaulked.

Most shops now wedge-seam the topsides and caulk only the bottom; in fact, some wedge the entire hull.

The wedged seam is a development made possible by the advent of waterproof glue and is the invention of an ingenious Scotsman named James Chambers.

The wedges are run on a ripsaw, dipped in a small trough of glue and then driven home. They should be of some soft wood such as cedar and of a length easy to handle, five to six feet. To save labor, they should be roughly trimmed off before the glue hardens. The seam is generally made as the plank is gotten out, though some shops have a circular cutter or saw that routs it out after the boat is planked. This of course makes a very neat uniform seam.

Many boats built in the damp Pacific Northwest wound up in the warm climate of Southern California or Florida without their seams cracking, though one sent to a desert lake experienced considerable trouble.

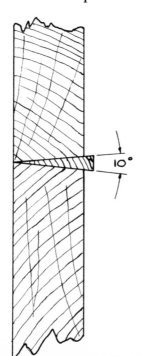

FIG. 14. Wedged seam

WEDGED SEAM

FIG. 15. Wedged seam

CLASSIFICATION OF BOAT-BUILDING WOODS

The following is a general classification of boat-building woods as to purpose for which they are used in boat construction.

KEEL—oak, Douglas fir, yellow and some of the other pines; also, in smaller boats, mahogany.

STEM—preferably hardwood: teak, oak, ironbark, bagac, hopea, and some of the gum woods; and on smaller craft, mahogany.

PLANKING—cypress, Western red, Port Orford, Alaska and white cedars, Philippine mahogany, and white pine. Runabouts and similar craft are often planked with Honduras and African mahogany. Spanish cedar, which finishes very much like mahogany, is also used where weight is a major consideration. West Coast work boats are generally planked with Oregon pine, but in fresh water it does not last very long. It should not be used for planking much less than 1¼″ thick.

Planking must be clear, and Douglas fir, red cedar, white pine, and some of the other soft woods should be vertical grain, as it is harder and shrinks and swells less. Wide planks on the topside should be avoided, though in batten seam construction it is not practical to have them too narrow.

FRAMES—For steam bending, white oak is of course the only western wood, and it should be what is termed bending oak flat grain only (see Fig. 40). It is also excellent for sawed frames, as also are mahogany and the harder Alaska or yellow cedar. Spruce and other soft woods are often used where lightness is desired, but they do not hold fastenings well, and larger fastenings, or preferably screw fastenings, should be used to compensate for this. Material for sawed frames need not be clear, as knots, if they are not too numerous, may be worked out in cutting up the material.

STRINGERS, CLAMPS and SHELF—Douglas fir, yellow pine, white oak, and Port Orford and Alaska cedar are also used for shelves, particularly where the deck is laid directly upon the shelf, as this form of construction affords rather inadequate ventilation and dry rot is likely to occur.

DECKING—for caulked decks: teak, mahogany, Port Orford, white, and Alaska cedar, white pine, and Douglas fir; the last two must be vertical grain. For adequate caulking and in any but the lightest jobs, the single thickness deck should not be much less than 1¼″ thick, and the widths should be kept to about double the thickness. The plank deck laid over plywood is strong and almost leakproof.

Where decks are to be fiberglassed or covered with some similar fabric they should be of waterproof plywood (as should all other plywood). Many builders glue it also to shelf beams and headers, making for a very strong structure.

DECK BEAMS—white oak, Douglas fir, yellow pine, mahogany, and Alaska or yellow cedar; in very light construction, spruce.

FLOOR TIMBERS—white oak, Douglas fir, yellow pine and sometimes Alaska cedar. These need not be clear, as a few knots will do no harm.

TRANSOMS—As these are usually finished bright or varnished, teak or mahogany is generally used. For a painted job any of the planking woods are suitable, as it is, of course, just the after planking of the boat. Sailboat transoms are generally sawed to shape and often faced with hardwood; some rot-resisting material should be used for the back or sawed part.

SEAM BATTENS—spruce, Port Orford and yellow cedar, oak, and mahogany.

CABIN TRUNKS—teak, mahogany, and Spanish cedar if finished bright, and red, Alaska, Port Orford cedar, and cypress for a painted job, and of course plywood.

GUARDS—ironbark, Australian gum, bagac, and some other hardwoods. Oak is often used but is not the best material. Teak and mahogany have a very nice appearance but lack the desired hardness. However, they may be faced with half oval metal.

MASTS and SPARS—Spruce is of course the finest material obtainable for this purpose, combining strength with lightness. Douglas fir and some of the pines are often used but seldom for hollow sticks.

THE LUMBER ORDER

Hardwoods are generally stocked in the rough and surfaced to order; the same applies to the cedars. Douglas fir and pine are obtainable direct from the mill or yard in the surfaced state and are seldom stocked otherwise.

In purchasing rough lumber ¼″ is allowed for surfacing two sides. If it has been carefully sawed, however, it is not necessary to lose more than ⅛″ in surfacing, and it is sometimes possible to get ¹⁵⁄₁₆″ out of a 1″ board. A ⅞″ board should be obtainable from 1″ stock.

Following is a table (Fig. 16) showing standard surfaced or finished dimensions for Douglas fir lumber and the rough size each is obtained from, for which you pay in purchasing.

You can, of course, obtain net sizes surfaced, but it is always cheaper to use stock sizes. Planking is often ordered S2S, or surfaced two sides only, as this additional width can be used to advantage.

Common symbols used by lumbermen to designate surfacing, etc., are S1S, S2S, S2S1E, and so forth, meaning surfaced one side, surfaced two sides, and surfaced both sides and one edge. V.G. means vertical grain, B.M. board measure, and V.J. indicates a V joint in ceiling material.

Where strength and durability are required, air-seasoned stock is superior to kiln-dried unless special slow-drying treatment is used. The heat of the dry kiln destroys some of the life and bending qualities of the lumber, making it unsuited for planking or for any purpose that requires bending. By purchasing planking at the start of the job and stacking it with sticks between so that there is a free circulation of air, the builder usually has time to season green planking lumber before he is ready to use it. Stringers, shelves and clamps are not so important, and green bending oak is an advantage.

FASTENINGS

All fastenings used in boat building must be galvanized or of some corrosion-resisting metal such as bronze, copper, monel, or other alloy. Bolts, because of their size, are almost always of galvanized mild steel, and carriage bolts of this material can be purchased in most any size and length. Exceptionally long bolts can be made up of galvanized rod with a nut on one end and a clinch ring on the other. The galvanized bolt, being rough, is really superior for use as a drift bolt. A drift bolt is one driven into a tight hole, and its holding power is dependent upon the friction between bolt and wood.

The general practice is to allow ¹⁄₁₆″ for drift, boring a ⁷⁄₁₆″ hole for a ½″ bolt. Where a clinch ring is used on top the hole may be bored even size through the top or first piece. The bottom end should be "pointed" slightly with a hammer so that the bolt will follow the hole. Note: A nut and washer may be substituted if clinch rings are not available.

NAILS

Nail fastenings are of two types, round and square. The square or boat nail is always used for planking and the round or wire nail elsewhere. The boat nail is

FIG. 16

PLANK THICKNESS

ROUGH	FINISHED
1 ″	$^{11}/_{16}$″
1 ″	$^{25}/_{32}$″
1$^{1}/_{4}$″	1$^{1}/_{16}$″
1$^{1}/_{2}$″	1$^{5}/_{16}$″
2 ″	1$^{5}/_{8}$ ″
2$^{1}/_{2}$″	2$^{1}/_{8}$ ″
3 ″	2$^{5}/_{8}$ ″
3$^{1}/_{2}$″	3$^{1}/_{8}$ ″
4 ″	3$^{5}/_{8}$ ″

PLANK WIDTHS

ROUGH	FINISHED
2″	1$^{5}/_{8}$″
3″	2$^{5}/_{8}$″
4″	3$^{5}/_{8}$″
6″	5$^{5}/_{8}$″
8″	7$^{1}/_{2}$″
10″	9$^{1}/_{2}$″
12″	11$^{1}/_{2}$″
and so forth	

FIG. 17

NAILS—NUMBER IN POUNDS

PENNY	LENGTH IN INCHES	GALV. BOAT	GALV. WIRE	COPPER BOAT
	$^{3}/_{4}$	500	800	800
	$^{7}/_{8}$	450	700	600
2	1	400	550	495
3	1$^{1}/_{4}$	300	400	320
4	1$^{1}/_{2}$	200	260	215
5	1$^{3}/_{4}$	135	170	155
6	2	95	110	115
7	2$^{1}/_{4}$	68	80	85
8	2$^{1}/_{2}$	50	70	65
10	3	33	57	44
12	3$^{1}/_{4}$	28	50	37
16	3$^{1}/_{2}$	24	43	30
20	4	20	30	20

SCREW SIZES IN INCHES

SIZE NO.	DIA. OF SHANK	DIA. OF HEAD	SIZE NO.	DIA. OF SHANK	DIA. OF HEAD
4	.109″ or $^{1}/_{8}$″	$^{1}/_{4}$″	14	.241″ or $^{1}/_{4}$″	$^{1}/_{2}$″
6	.135″ or $^{9}/_{64}$″	$^{5}/_{16}$″	16	.268″ or $^{9}/_{32}$″	$^{9}/_{16}$″
8	.162″ or $^{11}/_{64}$″	$^{11}/_{32}$″	18	.293″ or $^{5}/_{16}$″	$^{5}/_{8}$″
10	.188″ or $^{3}/_{16}$″	$^{3}/_{8}$″	24	.374″ or $^{3}/_{8}$″	$^{3}/_{4}$″
12	.215″ or $^{7}/_{32}$″	$^{7}/_{16}$″	28	.427″ or $^{7}/_{16}$″	$^{7}/_{8}$″

made in two forms, the blunt point and the chisel point. The latter is the better and should be driven so that the chisel point cuts the grain of the wood. These nails have such holding power that when removing planking for a repair job, the nails pull through the plank and remain sticking out of the frame. The galvanized nail has the additional advantage in that the longer it remains in the wood the tighter its hold becomes. However, after a few years some of the nails "bleed" through the paint and eventually the strength of the fastening itself becomes impaired, though this may take as long as thirty to fifty years.

Nonferrous nails, bronze and monel, have largely replaced the galvanized. Care should be taken in ordering these in the longer sizes, as many, if not most, are of too thin a wire for their length and have impaired shearing properties, allowing the plank to work. As a guide, a two-inch nail should be about as thick as its galvanized round nail counterpart, or ⅛" +.

SCREWS

Brass or composition screws are superior to the galvanized iron in that the threads are sharper and clear cut. This is not so important in the larger sizes, but any thread up to about 1½" No. 12 had best be brass or bronze. Brass contains a large content of zinc and should not be used outside where submerged in salt water where it is gradually destroyed by galvanic action. Bronze, monel, Everdure, or similar metals are proof against this action.

For light work and where fastening into butt blocks, soft wood frames, and seam battens, the screw plank fastening is superior to nailing.

3/ LOFTING OR "LAYING DOWN"

THIS, THE FIRST STEP IN BUILDING THE BOAT, is perhaps the most difficult, though not as mysterious or complicated as some would lead us to believe. In reality it consists in enlarging the "lines drawing" to full size on the mold loft floor. Accuracy is essential, and a little care and effort will save much labor later on in the construction of the boat. It should be mentioned here that each step in this chapter, as for instance laying out the transom, should be read entirely through before work is begun to ascertain the proper procedure applying to the design on hand.

We will presume that the builder is in possession of the lines and offsets of the boat as drawn by a naval architect and laid out in the usual manner. The first requisite is a smooth surface upon which to enlarge these lines. The boat shop has a mold loft especially for this purpose. Any smooth flat surface of sufficient size, however, will do. The job will be made easier if the boat can be laid down in one length, but if this is not possible, a little more than half the length will do, superimposing the forward half over the after one with a few feet to spare for overlap.

For the amateur who lays down but one boat, a platform may be built of some of the planking lumber, or if a floor is available this may be covered with light-colored building paper. One-quarter-inch plywood panels of the poorest grade, called rejects, make an ideal floor and are not very expensive. One advantage of building paper is that it can be saved for future use, though it is not a very desirable surface to work on.

Three views of the hull lines are shown in Fig. 18. They are usually arranged as in Fig. 19. The two upper ones are elevations, the profile or longitudinal side view, and the body plan which is a series of cross sections through the hull; as both sides of the boat are alike, the forward half is shown on the right and the aft end on the left side of a common centerline. The lower plan is the half breadth or plan view showing the shape of waterlines and deck line on one

25

side and the diagonals on the other. Diagonals are often dispensed with in V-bottom lines. On the mold loft floor the three views are superimposed one over the other as shown in Fig. 20, and the base line becomes the centerline for half breadth and diagonals.

METHOD OF PROCEDURE

I have chosen as an example a small power boat (Fig. 20) and a small sailboat (Fig. 18). A sailboat with its curved, sloping transom involves certain difficulties and is the most intricate to lay out.

The first procedure is to lay out the straight lines. Use a chalk line for this and start with the base line, and parallel above it place the waterlines and buttocks as in Fig. 20; in this case W.L. 21″ and the buttock happen to coincide. This is not generally the case, and two or three buttocks are usually shown. Strike in the diagonals and buttocks in the body plan, also the stations for the profile and half breadth as spaced in the drawing. Harden up all these lines using pencil and straight-edge.

BATTENS

From this point on you will require some battens—for the longitudinal lines at least one the full length of the job, with two or three feet overlength. Their size will depend on the length of the boat and sharpness of the curves. For the small cruiser use one about 1¼″ square tapered at one end to about ¾″ x 1¼″ or even smaller for the sharp curve of the deck line. It is nice to have two battens, one flat about ⅜″ or ½″ x 1½″ or 2″ for the straighter lines, and it can be used later in running sheer line on the boat and in planking. It is often difficult to secure these in one length, and two shorter pieces can be glued together satisfactorily, using a long scarf. All battens must be fair and without kinks. The body plan and the buttocks forward will require some smaller battens, and their size will depend upon the sharpness of the bilge. They may have to be as small as ⅜″ x ½″ to make the sharp curve on the transom of some power boats. Two or three should be made, as you are almost sure to break one. Oak is about the only material that will stand the bend, though it has the disadvantage of keeping the kink after bending. Pine, fir, or cedar will be best for long battens. Do not drive nails directly into any but a wide batten, as the nail holes weaken it and it will soon break.

Beneath the base line is nailed a base batten (it need not be in one length) as shown in Fig. 20, and all measurements are taken by butting the rule against it, which facilitates the job greatly. A short straight-edge may later be tacked alongside the body plan centerline and shifted from side to side, depending on which end of the boat you are working on as shown.

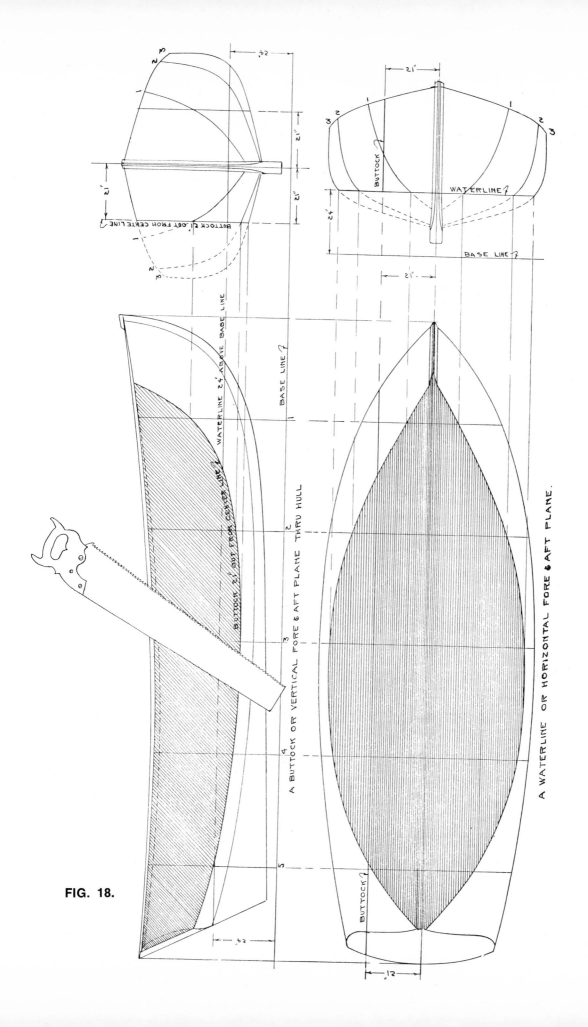

FIG. 18.

A BUTTOCK OR VERTICAL FORE & AFT PLANE THRU HULL

A WATERLINE OR HORIZONTAL FORE & AFT PLANE.

BASE LINE

WATERLINE 24" ABOVE BASE LINE

BUTTOCK 21" OUT FROM CENTER LINE

BUTTOCK 21" OUT FROM CENTER LINE

BASE LINE

WATERLINE

BUTTOCK

BUTTOCK

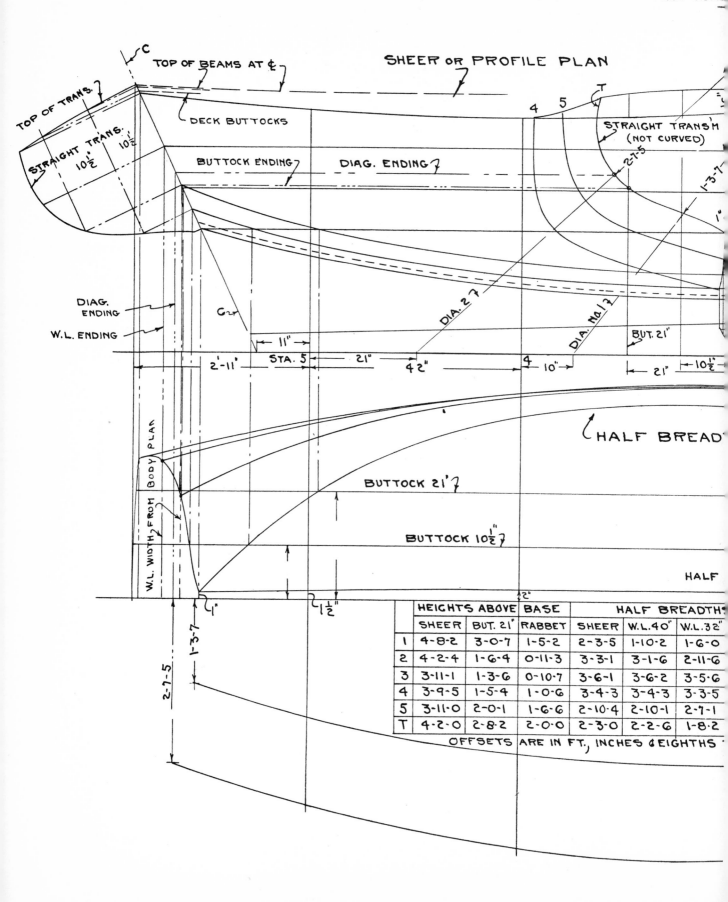

SHEER OR PROFILE PLAN

TOP OF TRANS.

TOP OF BEAMS AT ₵

DECK BUTTOCKS

STRAIGHT TRANS. 10½"   10½"

STRAIGHT TRANS'M (NOT CURVED)

BUTTOCK ENDING

DIAG. ENDING

2-7-5

1-3-7

DIAG. ENDING

W.L. ENDING

C₂

DIA. 2.7

DIA. No. 2

BUT. 21"

11"

2'-11"   STA. 5   21"   4 2"   4   10"   21"   10½"

HALF BREAD

BODY PLAN

BUTTOCK 21'

BUTTOCK 10½"

W.L. WIDTH FROM

HALF

1"   1½"   2"

HALF

2-7-5   1-3-7

OFFSETS ARE IN FT., INCHES & EIGHTHS

	HEIGHTS ABOVE BASE			HALF BREADTH		
	SHEER	BUT. 21"	RABBET	SHEER	W.L.40"	W.L. 32"
1	4-8-2	3-0-7	1-5-2	2-3-5	1-10-2	1-6-0
2	4-2-4	1-6-4	0-11-3	3-3-1	3-1-6	2-11-6
3	3-11-1	1-3-6	0-10-7	3-6-1	3-6-2	3-5-6
4	3-9-5	1-5-4	1-0-6	3-4-3	3-4-3	3-3-5
5	3-11-0	2-0-1	1-6-6	2-10-4	2-10-1	2-7-1
T	4-2-0	2-8-2	2-0-0	2-3-0	2-2-6	1-8-2

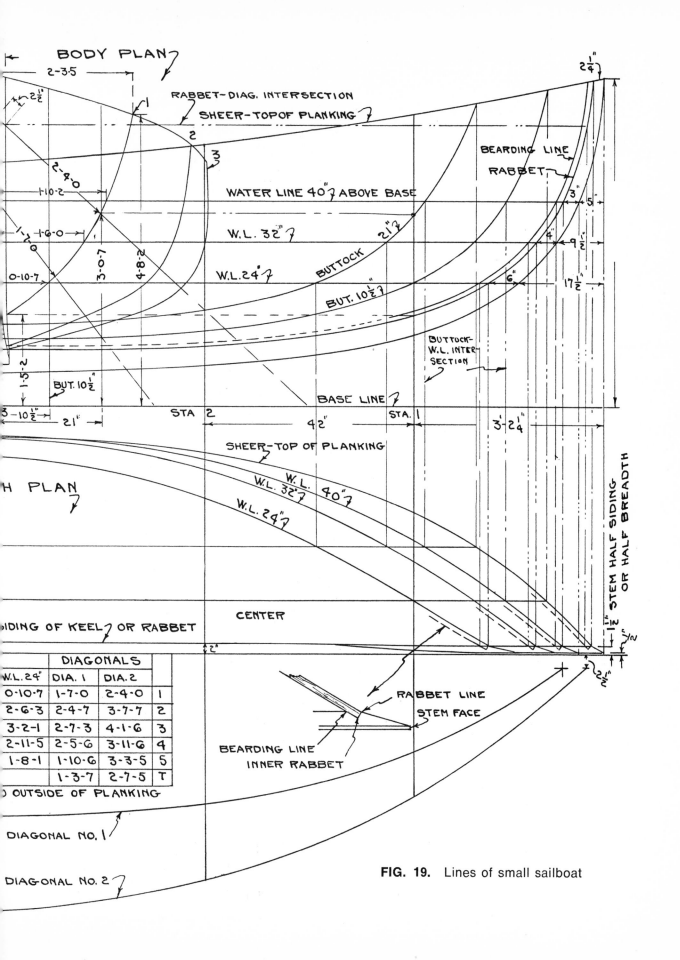

FIG. 19. Lines of small sailboat

FIG. 20. Lines of small power boat

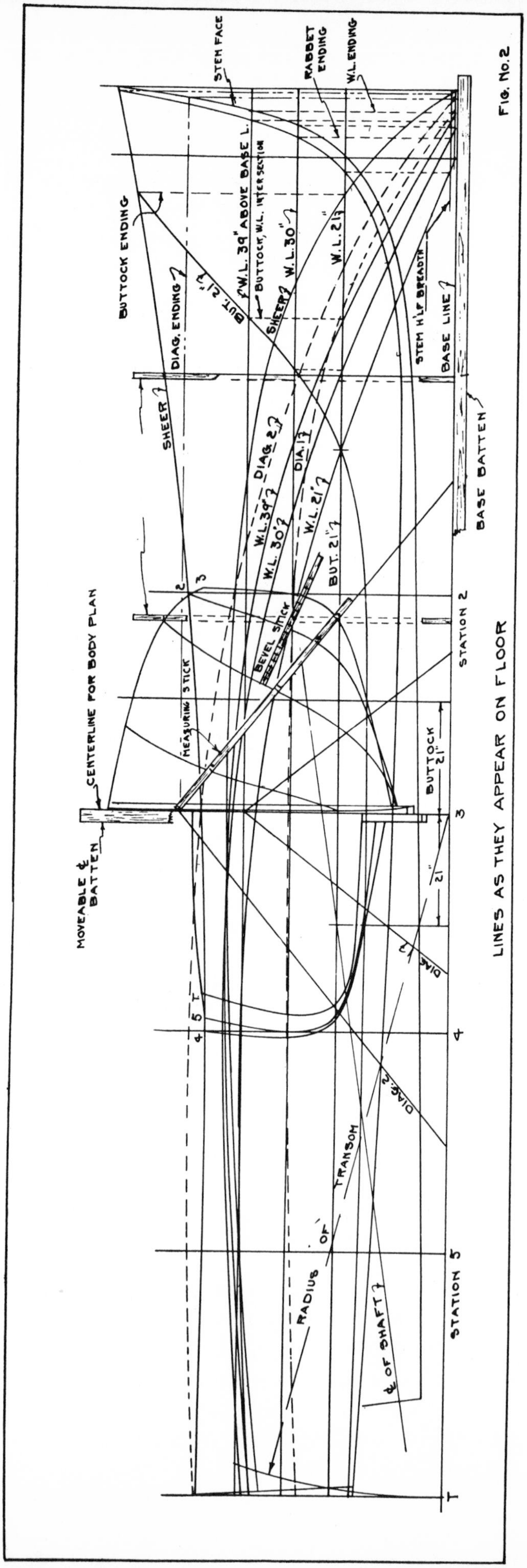

LAYING DOWN THE BOAT

From this point there are several methods of procedure, but I believe it is best first to lay out those lines that will not have to be altered later on. These are usually the sheer line in half breadth and profile, the stem face and keel bottom, and in some boats the entire rabbet line. The entire rabbet line would be run in in Fig. 19, for instance, as the waterlines do not fair into the stem face. In Fig. 20 the rabbet would be run in from station No. 1 aft, as the true rabbet forward will be obtained later and would only have to be corrected if run in now.

To describe how these lines are run in we will take the profile sheer line in Fig. 19. Turning to heights above base line in the offsets and butting your rule against the base line batten, mark on station 1 the height 4′ 8¼″; station 2, 4′ 2½″; and so on to the height at the stem. At each of these spots drive a finish nail and place the batten against these nails with a nail on the opposite side, to hold it in place. There will no doubt be some discrepancies and hard spots, so shift the batten to suit, giving and taking so that it takes a fair curve without lumps or flat spots. This is called fairing up, and the batten should be sprung so that the convex or outside of the curve is against the nails.

THE BODY PLAN

The body plan is next. Draw in the stem, keel, and horn timber half width, or half siding, as it is termed. With most boats these will be straight lines, though in a hollow keel sailboat the keel rabbet will show curved, as in Fig. 22.

In Fig. 19, station 1, is shown how the offsets are applied from the table of offsets to the floor. Do not, however, use these measurements for the sheer or rabbet, but transfer them from the lines you have already faired up on the floor. Use a small batten about ¼″ x 1″ for this. Tack the temporary batten against the body plan centerline, Fig. 20, and butting the measuring stick against the base line on station 1, mark the sheer and rabbet heights and sheer width, and transfer these to the body plan. Tack finish nails on all the spots and spring a batten to the shape, fairing it up as before. Do not mark these lines in permanently but either lightly with a pencil or, if the surface is suitable, use a piece of soapstone.

FAIRING UP THE LINES

With the body plan marked in we can start fairing up these lines. Citing Figs. 19 and 20, I would run in first the diagonals as they intersect the station lines almost at right angles. Place the measuring stick against the centerline as in Fig. 20 and mark the diagonal width of stem face as well as each station crossing. Now to end the diagonal forward, transfer the height at which it intersects the stem face or rabbet half siding on the body plan to the stem face forward (Fig. 20); then square this distance down to the stem face half siding at the base line. Measure the diagonal width of stem face out on this line and it will be the diagonal ending. The diagonal ending aft, with a plumb station T as in Fig. 20, is the same as a station ending, but with the sloping transom as in Fig. 19 the same procedure is followed as forward, except of course that the transom diagonal distance is laid off instead of stem face half siding. Spot each diagonal distance on each station and spring the long batten to these spots, shifting it here and there to form a fair line. Mark this line in lightly and correct the body plan to suit.

WATERLINES AND BUTTOCKS

The waterlines had probably best be run in next. The method of ending these lines is clearly shown, and the stem face intersection in the profile is transferred down to the stem face next to the base line. All discrepancies in the body plan are changed as each line is run in.

The buttock lines must intersect the waterlines in the profile at the same point they intersect in the half breadth, and the method used in obtaining these intersections is shown in both Figs. 19 and 20, transferring the intersections in the half breadth to the waterlines in the profile. The height of buttock-transom intersection in body plan is transferred aft to the transom in the profile as shown in Fig. 19. So far in referring to the transom in profile, we refer to the straight line marked C-C in Fig. 19 and not to the curved lines which will be developed later.

In the process of fairing up the body plan, considerable shifting of lines is bound to occur. To make all the lines conform and still produce lines that are fair and pleasing to the eye, the changing of one will sometimes affect two or three others, and until the last line is run in one never knows just how nearly finished one is.

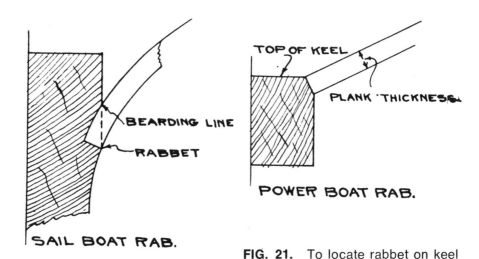

BEARDING LINE

RABBET

SAIL BOAT RAB.

TOP OF KEEL

PLANK THICKNESS

POWER BOAT RAB.

FIG. 21. To locate rabbet on keel

FIG. 22.
Sailboat lines

	HEIGHTS ABOVE BASE					HALF BREADTHS									DIAGONALS			
	UNDER RAIL	BUT. 18"	BUT. 9"	RABETT	KEEL BOT.	UNDER RAIL	W.L. 6'9"	W.L. 6'-0"	W.L. 5'-3"	W.L. 4'-6"	W.L. 3'-9"	W.L. 3'-0"	W.L. 2'-3"	KEEL BOT.	DIA. 1	DIA. 2	DIA 3	
1	9-3-7	7-11-5	6-3-0	5-5-3	5-2-0	1-9-2	1-0-0	0-7-1	0-1-0							1-3-6	1-7-3	1
2	8-10-6	5-3-3	4-4-5	3-9-2	3-6-0	3-0-0	2-4-3	1-11-7	1-5-5	0-10-1	0-2-5			0-0-4	[illegible]			
3	8-6-7	4-0-0	3-2-6	2-9-1	2-2-2	3-10-3	3-5-4	3-1-7	2-8-2	2-0-2	1-2-7	0-6-7	0-2-2					
4	8-4-0	3-3-4	2-6-0	2-3-1	0-11-5	4-4-7	4-2-5	4-0-1	3-7-5	3-0-0	2-1-1	[illegible]						
5	8-2-1	3-0-5	2-3-2	2-0-6	0-3-3	4-7-6	4-7-3	4-5-7	4-2-4	[illegible]								
6	8-1-4	3-2-3	2-5-2	1-11-1	0-1-3	4-7-6	4-8-0	4-6-7	[illegible]									
7	8-0-7	3-8-4	3-1-6	2-0-0	5/8" BELOW	4-5-1	[illegible]											
8	8-0-2	4-6-4	4-1-6	3-4-5	2 3/4 "	[illegible]												
9	8-1-2	5-7-1	5-4-1	5-2-2	[illegible]													
10	[illegible]																	

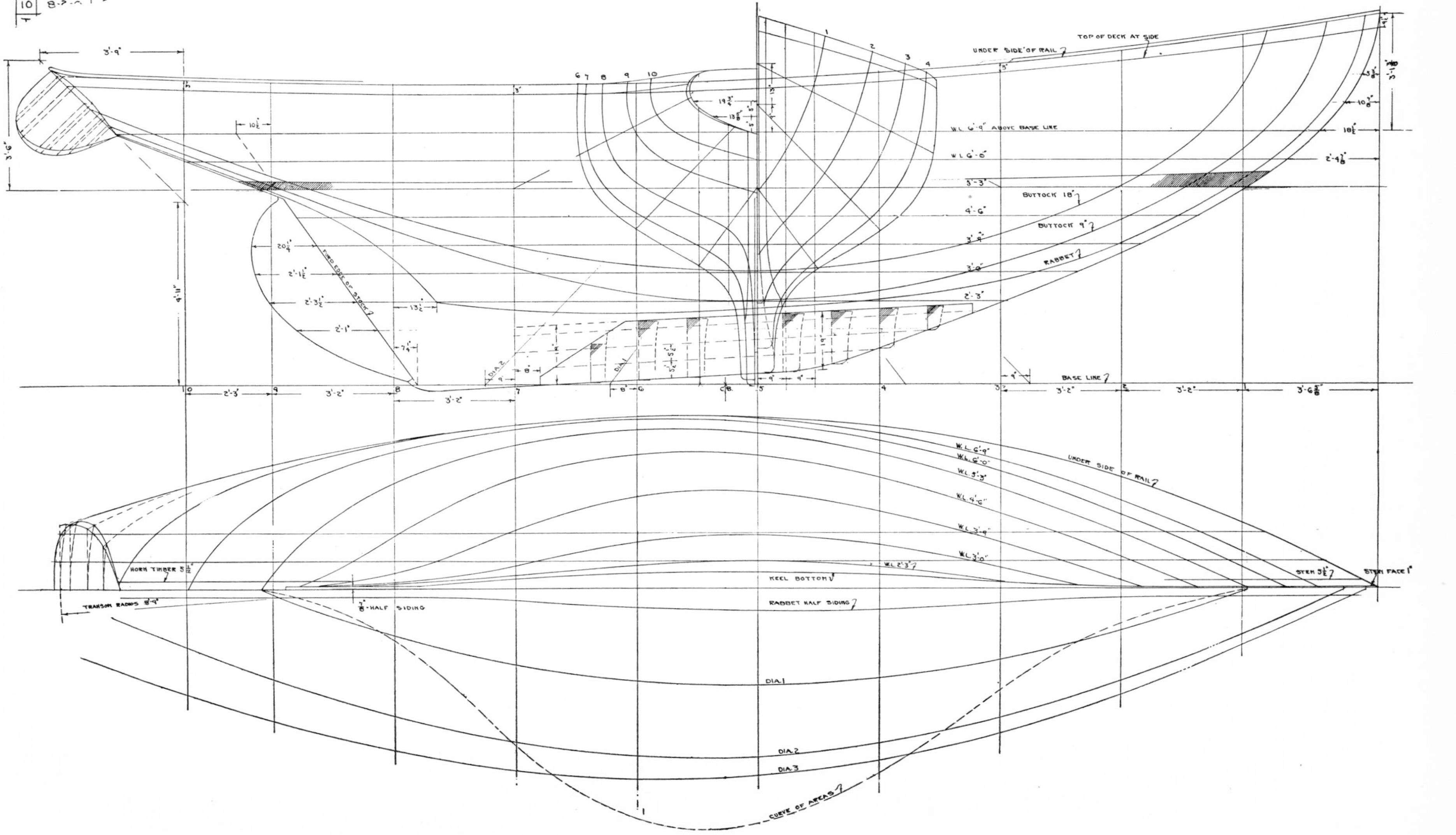

THE RABBET AND BEARDING LINE

The vessel's lines as indicated in the lines drawing are now all run in and faired up, and the various details such as rabbet, transom, etc., now remain. If, as in most power boats, the waterlines fair into the stem face as in Fig. 20, the location of the rabbet in the profile is obtained by squaring up the stem half breadth-waterline intersections in the half breadth to the sheer or profile waterlines as shown, and a thin batten is sprung through these spots and faired into the keel rabbet.

The bearding line is obtained by laying off the plank thickness on the half breadth waterlines and transferring the stem half breadth and plank thickness intersections up to the waterlines in the profile as in Fig. 19.

DEDUCTING FOR PLANK THICKNESS

Turning our attention to the body plan, we must deduct the plank thickness and thus obtain the outside of the frames and mark these in permanently. Some builders simply deduct this thickness directly on the body plan. This is of course correct amidships, where the lines are practically parallel to the centerline, but not exactly so forward and aft. A more exact method is first to lay off on these stations the plank thickness at the diagonals and sheer (half breadth plan) and then deduct the distance shown on the station line as in Fig. 23. When no diagonals are used, as in a V-bottom design, it is quite close enough to use the waterlines and buttocks instead. The exact plank thickness may be deducted at the rabbet, as there is little difference here. The top of the keel in power boats or the bearding line on the keel in most sailboats is obtained at each station, as in Fig. 21.

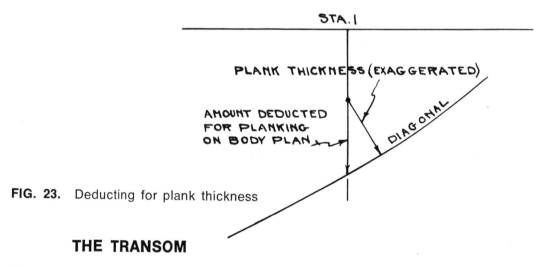

FIG. 23. Deducting for plank thickness

THE TRANSOM

The power-boat transom is a comparatively simple matter, and if it is not curved another station is struck in at the forward side of the transom frame, a mold or form made, and the frame bent just aft of it as any other frame in the boat.

A curved transom is a bit more difficult; the method of laying this out is shown in Fig. 24. The rake of the transom is struck in and the planking and frame thickness deducted. Each intersection of the for'd side of frame with sheer and waterlines is projected down to base line and the prescribed radius drawn in

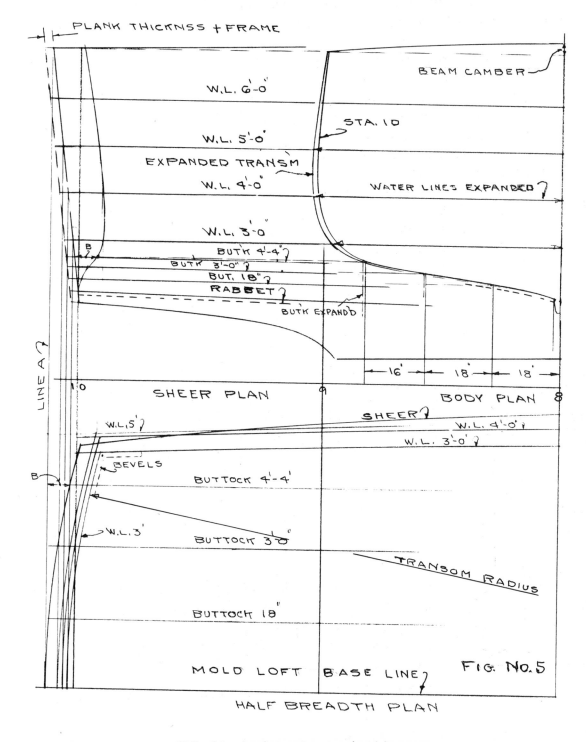

FIG. 24. Laying out power boat transom

from these points. From the half breadth plan obtain the amount of shape or curve at each buttock (Dimension B for 4′-4″ buttock). Transfer this up to the sheer plan. You can then draw in shape of bottom in this view, though it is not really necessary. Now parallel these intersections over to body plan and to the buttocks as shown in the light line above buttock 4′-4″.

The hull plank thickness is next deducted at each W.L., at sheer half breadth and at buttocks. The curved transom is next drawn in the body plan to the inside of plank, but instead of taking the dimensions square off the base line they are measured along the curve of the transom and then expanded on the body plan. The reason for expanding the transom is that the pattern must be made from this line later and sprung over a curved form.

The buttocks in body plan are expanded in the same manner. Should the transom have considerable rake, the distance between waterlines will have to be increased by taking the distances along transom rake and, starting at rabbet, increasing the spaces accordingly. With moderate rake as in Fig. 24 the change in W.L. spacing will be found to be almost nil and can be disregarded.

Figure 25 shows how the curved power-boat transom is built over a curved form. The transom pattern is laid on the form, the width of frame deducted, and cleats fastened in place against which the frame is bent. The transom should be planked before removing from form.

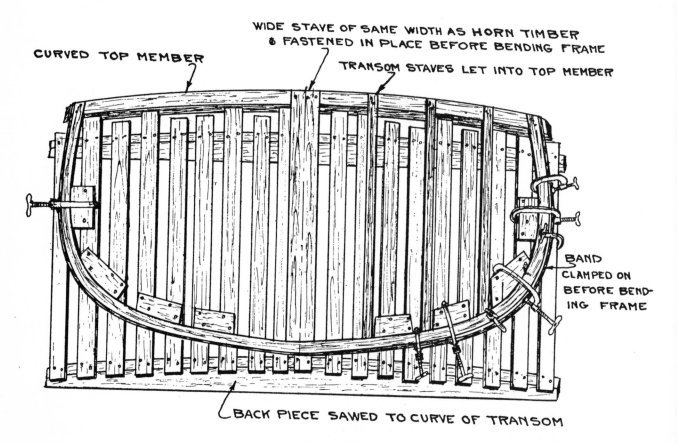

FIG. 25. Transom form

There is really another method employing less labor and less skill; however, a regular station or form must be employed just forward of the transom, and after all the ribbands, shelf, etc., are in place the transom top member is fastened in place. As there is generally a cockpit floor support, this is also set in place, and if none exists, a false one is substituted, allowing for the rake of the transom and using the aforementioned form to measure from.

Next a straight-edge is applied vertically to mark the curve at each ribband. You now have the shape of the transom, and if more points seem advisable, a few short ribbands can be fastened in place.

It would be a bit difficult, though not impossible, to bend in the transom frame, so it is generally sawed, as in Fig. 26.

The curved sloping sailboat transom is doubtless the most difficult problem in laying out that a boat builder will encounter. There are several methods used in laying this out, and architects have several methods of indicating the lines on the plan. Winslow places a perpendicular station aft of the transom, and all lines terminate here. Most architects, however, end the lines as in Figs. 19 and 27. Again, some show the transom radius on the waterline plane and others a radius square off the transom face.

Sailboat transoms are generally sawed to shape out of heavy material, and often a thin layer of hardwood is bent on the outside for a finish.

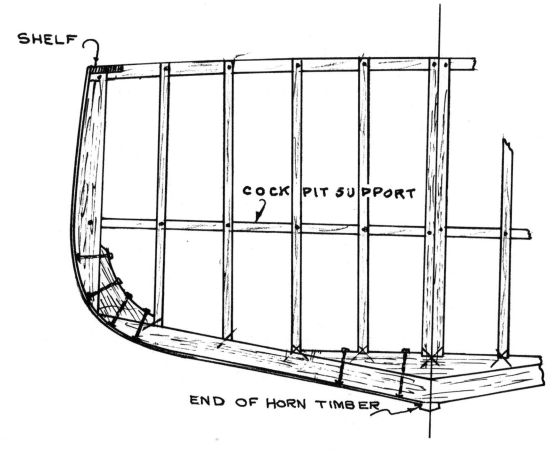

FIG. 26. Sawn transom

STRAIGHT SAILBOAT TRANSOM

In laying out the aft end of the boat the straight face line C-C, Fig. 19, is first laid out and the intersections of the various waterlines and deck line with this line squared down to the half breadth plan. The widths at these points will be taken from the widths of the various waterlines in the body plan as shown in Fig. 19; diagonals are ended as shown in this figure.

The next step is to lay out the transom from line C-C, which will give the true shape of the straight transom. We are really not much concerned with the shape above the deckline, as this part is usually put on after the vessel is decked, being part of the rail chock, so square out the deckline, waterlines, and buttocks from centerline C-C and strike in the straight buttocks their proper distance out from the centerline as shown (10½" in Fig. 19, 9" in Fig. 27).

From the body plan obtain the transom widths for each waterline and the deckline, and through these spots and the buttock intersection squared out from C-C (Fig. 19) may be drawn the true shape of the straight face transom. We must now obtain the shape of the top edge to allow for the crown of the deck (though the top of transom may be left rough and trimmed to conform with the top of the beams when in place on the boat). It is necessary, however, to first lay out the crown of the beams; this is shown and explained in Fig. 29. From the deck line in half breadth obtain the deck width at transom, also widths at stations 4 and 5, and transfer these to the beam camber as shown in Fig. 30, thus obtaining camber or crown of deck at each point.

Returning to Fig. 19, we can now draw in the top of beams on sheer plan. Again referring to Fig. 30: the buttocks are laid out and their distance down from centerline transferred to Fig. 19 and buttocks drawn in. The intersections of these lines with line C-C are squared out to the various corresponding buttocks, and a line through these intersections will produce the top of transom, Figs. 19 and 28.

RADIUSED OR CURVED SAILBOAT TRANSOM

Layout of the curved or radiused transom is shown in Fig. 27. In this, an imaginary cylinder is passed through the buttocks and waterlines. Line C-C is extended upward as shown, stations 5, 6, and 7 projected parallel to it, and the centerline, buttocks, and transom radius drawn in. Each buttock is projected down from transom radius to intersect those below in profile. Projecting intersections of the waterlines and sheer with C-C down to plan view, shown at bottom of page, we can draw in the straight transom in plan view. This may be also shown in the designer's lines drawing.

Project the intersections of the waterlines and buttocks with cylinder face (top view) down to meet those in the profile and parallel to C-C; W.L. 7'-3" is

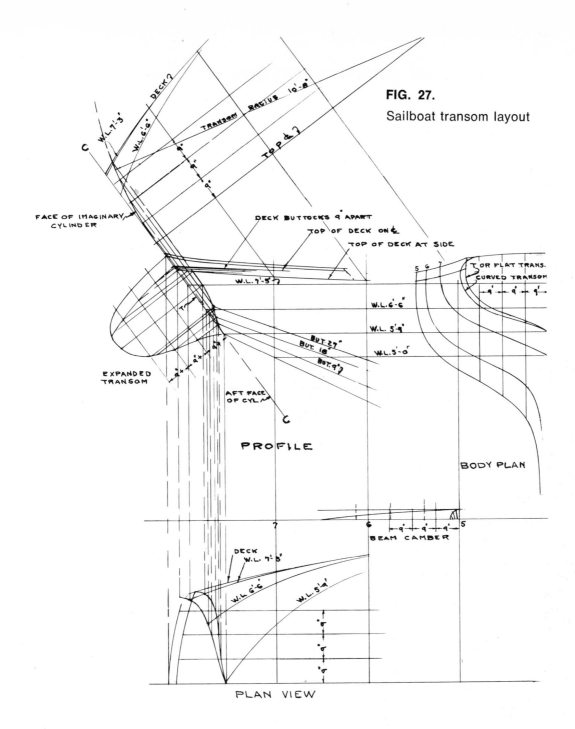

FIG. 27.

Sailboat transom layout

only W.L. thus shown. We can then draw in the radiused transom in the profile through the various intersections of buttocks and waterlines. Projecting the intersections down to plan view we obtain the widths at waterline and sheer, and these, with buttock intersections, enable one to lay out the curved transom in body plan.

We must now obtain the true shape of the curved transom in order to make a pattern which will produce the correct shape when laid on the transom timbers already sawed to transom radius. Springing a light batten on the face of our imaginary cylinder (top view), the expanded distances between the buttocks is obtained and laid out parallel to C-C shown as 9″ +. The waterlines must also be expanded by taking their widths on the body plan, applying them from the top or projected centerline to the transom radius or cylinder face and square off centerline; then, springing a light batten along the curve, apply it to each waterline and the sheer on the expanded transom. We now have a sufficient number of points to draw in the expanded transom. Projecting the deck buttocks to the expanded transom buttocks, the top of the transom may be arrived at.

The transom face will perhaps be covered with a thin thickness of teak or mahogany. This will make the boat a half inch or so longer, but should be of small moment and can, of course, be avoided if line C-C is moved forward to begin with.

FIG. 28. Sailboat transom and hull framing. Transom will later be faced with ½″ teak.

Photo by Ray Krantz

On a very nice job, this transom facing is put on after the boat is planked. The stub ends of hull planking are trimmed off on the inner side to present the same width all around the transom and the outer facing of transom fitted to this.

The radius or curve is sawed in the transom pieces first. One advantage in this is that several pieces may be sawed from one wide timber—for instance, the whole of a transom three feet long obtained from one piece, say 8″ x 10″ x 3′.

These pieces are roughly smoothed off and clamped together and the expanded pattern bent over the surface and the shape marked off. We must now deduct for hull planking and obtain the bevels. These may be obtained as per Fig. 43. Referring to Fig. 27, body plan, square up from station 7 and lay out distance between 7 and curved transom on square. Obtain distance between 7 and curved transom from profile, taking it at 90° off curved transom. Bevels at bottom of transom may be obtained from buttocks in profile, allowing a little wood for trimming off when in place. The bevels we have obtained cannot of course be applied directly to the curved surface, as they apply from the straight surface A-B, Fig. 31. An easy way to allow for this is to lay each piece on the bench convex or face up, and by reversing the bevel apply it from the bench as in Fig. 31. Plank thickness can be deducted as in Fig. 32. A spot or two on each piece is all that is required, and the pieces are then bolted together and the bevels faired up between the spots. The entire transom may be bolted together first and the bevels applied later, but it should be blocked up so that the centerline is parallel to the surface of the bench; otherwise the bevels as applied from the bench would not be correct.

NOTE— SCRIBE QUARTER CIRCLE WITH SAME RADIUS AS CROWN & DIVIDE BASE & CIRCUMFERENCE INTO 4 PARTS & DRAW LINES A, B & C BETWEEN POINTS. DIVIDE W-W INTO 8 EQUAL PARTS & ERECT PERPENDICULARS A, B & C WITH SAME HEIGHT AS LENGTH OF A, B & C IN CIRCLE & SPRING BATTEN THRU THESE POINTS.

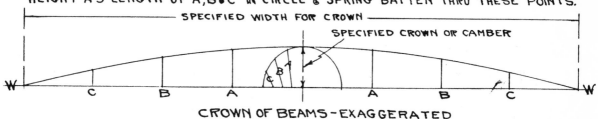

CROWN OF BEAMS-EXAGGERATED

FIG. 29. Beam crown

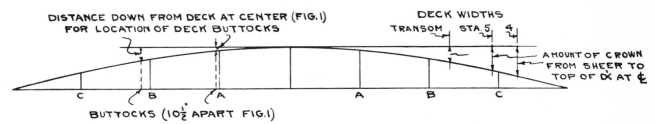

FIG. 30. Transom curve and crown

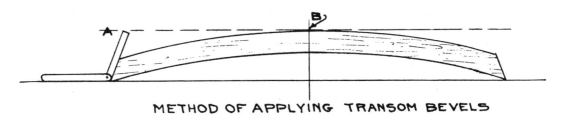

METHOD OF APPLYING TRANSOM BEVELS

FIG. 31. Transom bevels

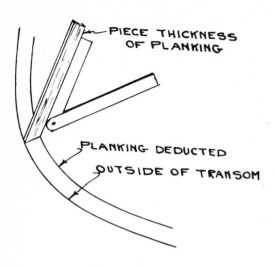

FIG. 32. Transom bevels

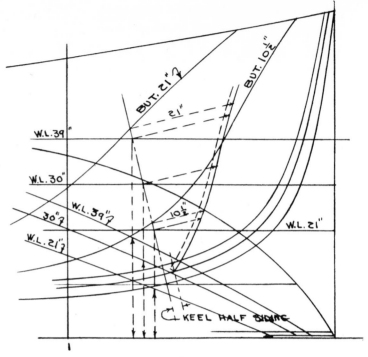

FIG. 33. To pass section through lines of hull

MISCELLANEOUS

There are two or three further details in lofting a boat that may at some time prove of value. It is possible to pass a section through almost any point of the boat and obtain the exact shape at this section. Fig. 33 shows a line or plane passed through the forefoot at right angles to the rabbet and how the shape of this section is obtained. The widths of each waterline intersection are obtained from the half breadth plan as shown. This cross-section was used in this case to locate more accurately the bearding line, as there is quite a space between station 1 and W.L. 21″.

The stations as located on the plan by the architect are for the purpose of showing and accurately outlining the shape of the hull. It sometimes happens that this location interferes with some of the frames, in which case it is an easy matter to strike in a new station or stations a few inches from their original position.

While the wood boat has been used as an example, the same principles apply to all the other types of construction—steel, ferro-cement, etc. With the steel or aluminum boat, however, the custom has been to neglect the skin thickness and not deduct it as with a wood boat. This of course makes the boat a little bit wider—so little, however, as to amount to about ½″ for a sixty-foot boat.

4/
MOLDS
AND PATTERNS

WE WILL ASSUME that the lines of the boat have been transferred from the scale drawing to full size on the mold loft floor and the process of laying down the boat completed. The next step will be to transfer these lines from floor to boat. This is done by the use of molds, or forms, as they are also called, and patterns. Molds are used in round-bottom construction and are to the shape of each station, with of course skin thickness deducted and sometimes the frames and ribbands also. Figure 40 shows such a form.

The different backbone members such as stem, keel, and horn timber are laid out on the floor and patterns or templates made of each (Fig. 34). A poor

FIG. 34. Making stem and backbone patterns. This apprentice is William Garden, world famous designer of power boats and sailboats.

Photo by Ray Krantz

grade of cedar or soft pine, ⁵⁄₁₆″ to ½″ thick, is ideal for the purpose. However, ¼″ plywood is almost universally now used for the purpose, and there is a very heavy pattern paper widely used in the large steel and aluminum shops. In transferring the lines from floor to pattern, tacks or nails are laid flat on the floor with heads on the line and with the body part at right angles to it. These are placed from two to three inches apart and the pattern lumber firmly pressed against the floor. The imprint of the tack head will be plainly marked, and by springing a batten through the spots, the shape of the part is obtained. Rabbet and bearding line are transferred in the same manner, not, however, until the pattern itself has been cut to shape. By drilling through pattern these lines are transferred to other side. In Fig. 35 a pattern would be made of the forward end of the keel back to about halfway between stations 2 and 3 and the balance of the keel represented by a batten with its lower edge at the bottom of the keel. The various stations are marked on the batten and the distances from keel bottom to top of keel, and the depths and width of the keel rabbet (see Fig. 36). At the aft end, the slope of the shaft log is marked or a pattern made of this and a separate pattern made of the horn timber. Fit all the various patterns together on the floor, making sure they fit together properly. The load waterline must be

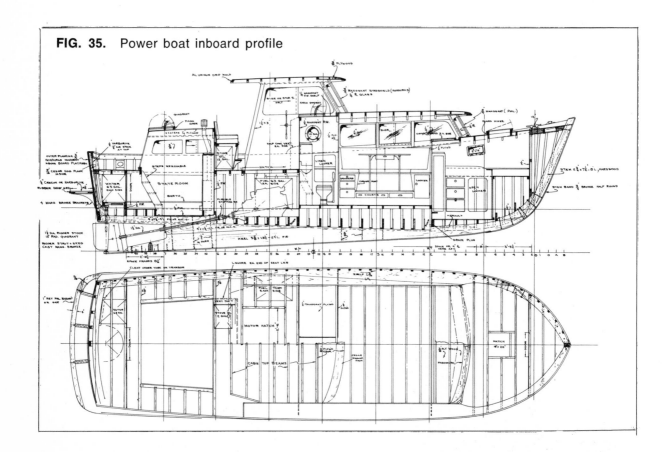

FIG. 35. Power boat inboard profile

marked on the stem pattern and where it applies, as in most sailboats, also marked on the horn timber. The location of the frames should also be marked on the patterns and later transferred to the keel, etc.

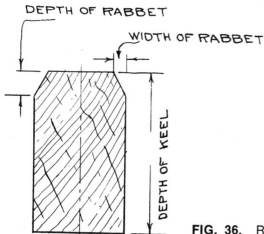

FIG. 36. Rabbet depths and widths and keel depths

The centerline of shaft is marked on the lines drawing, but both motor and wheel should be laid out to full size on the floor. Motor manufacturers supply an installation diagram, and from this the outline of the motor may be drawn in the profile. It is often found that the shaft line must be raised a little or the motor moved forward or aft slightly to clear properly, and the time to find this out is before and not after the hull is built. Make sure also that there is room to swing a propeller of proper diameter.

As the power boat's keel and backbone are of the same width or at least closely so from stem to stern, a shape of the side view or elevation is all that is needed. Not so, however, with the sailboat, especially with the modern keel boat, as shown in Fig. 23, where there is hardly a flat side surface, excepting stem and horn timber. Here it will be necessary to lay out keel and deadwood first in the profile and then their top and bottom surfaces in half breadth. This is a similar operation to laying out the various waterlines and should need no explanation. The rabbet half breadth is always given in the lines as well as width of keel bottom, and these are used when laying the sailboat down in obtaining the shape of the boat below the lowest waterline.

KEEL CASTING PATTERN

Outside ballast in sailers is usually in the form of a casting, either lead or iron, and a pattern must be made for this. A lead keel can be cast by the builder, in which case a mold is made of wood to the keel shape and the lead poured directly into it. For an iron casting, or if the lead keel is to be cast by a foundry, the metal keel is of course first represented by a wood pattern its exact shape, with allowance for shrinkage in casting. This amounts to ⅛″ per foot for iron and ³⁄₁₆″ for lead, and the pattern must be made larger by this amount.

The straight-sided and flat-bottom keel requires only a box to the proper dimensions, but a shaped keel, as in Fig. 23, will have to be built up in layers, each one sawed to shape before putting them together. Citing Fig. 23, three water-lines 5½″ apart from and parallel to the bottom were struck in, and three layers 5½″ and one 2¾″ for the top sawed to shape, with allowance of ⅛″ per foot, or 2½″ in length and ³⁄₁₆″ in height, for shrinkage. These were fastened together and planed smooth with lower corners rounded as shown. The position of bolts was marked, and the foundry took care of the core print, not overlooking a larger hole at bottom for the bolt heads.

THE LEAD KEEL

Had this casting been of lead and to be poured by the owner, the same principle would be used, except that a hollow mold would be made instead of a pattern. This is a more difficult job, and each layer is made of two pieces, one for starboard and the other for port, and fastened together at the ends and bottom (Fig. 37). Plaster of Paris may be used for fillets to form the rounded corners. To protect the mold from burning it is rubbed well with chalk, and some have tried papering the interior with light asbestos paper. The chalk or whitewash will burn through and scorch the wood, and the asbestos paper bulges out here and there, caused by the air expanding behind it. Some sort of heavy asbestos paint, if obtainable, would probably be better than either of the above.

Lead melts at the comparatively low temperature of a little over 600 degrees Fahrenheit, and a cast-iron pot, hot fire, and ladle are all the equipment needed.

The bolt holes are seldom allowed for in casting; instead they are drilled out later. An ordinary barefoot wood auger will cut through the lead almost as easily as through wood. The holes for the bolt heads may also be drilled if a large drill is obtainable; if not, they may be cut out with chisel and gouge.

THE CONCRETE KEEL

A great many builders are using concrete and boiler punchings for an inexpensive keel, and though inferior to cast iron, being lighter per cubic foot, these are quite practicable. Some use a welded steel casting and others pour the concrete in a form, much as is done in building construction, reinforcing it with steel rods. This is just as good. As the concrete keel really comes under construction, and as the making of a form should not require explanation, it will be covered later under erecting the boat.

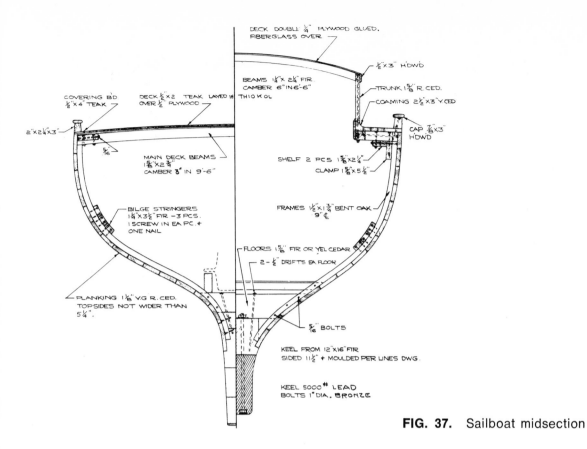

FIG. 37. Sailboat midsection

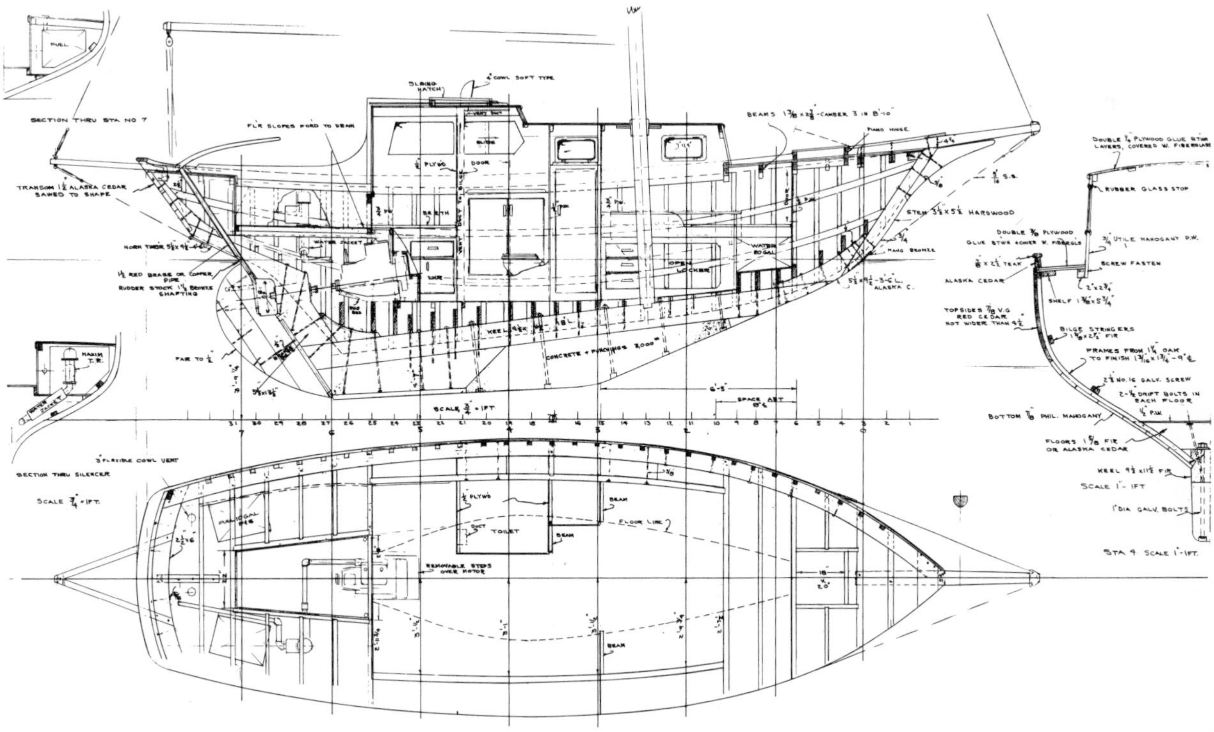

FIG. 38. Inboard profile and deck framing plan, 26-foot-keel sloop

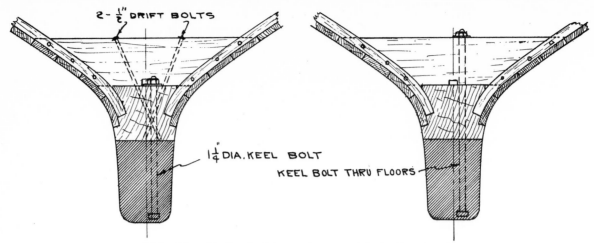

FIG. 39. Method of fastening outside ballast keels

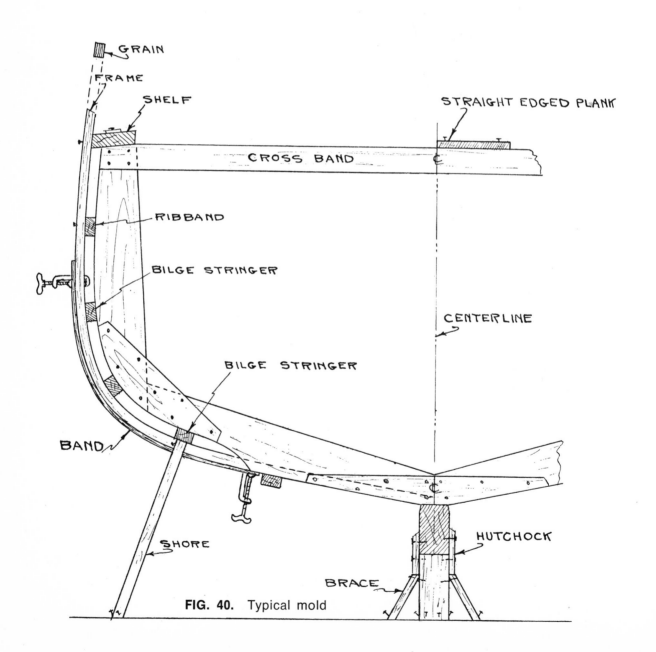

FIG. 40. Typical mold

KEEL FASTENINGS

There are two methods of fastening the keel casting to the boat, as shown in Fig. 39. Where possible it is much easier to fasten directly to the keel and not through the floors as shown on the right. With floor timbers well drift-bolted to the keel, this makes a good job, and great accuracy is not required in locating the bolt holes.

Where the keel bolts pass through the floor timbers, except with lead keels, the floors must be fitted over the bolts after the boat is set up, for iron keels, or each floor laid out in the mold loft and wood keel bolted in place through floors to metal keel before keel is set up. The latter is the craftsmanlike way of doing it but requires skill and accuracy and probably involves more labor.

MOLDS OR FORMS

So much for patterns. Figure 40 shows a typical mold set up on the keel with ribbands and frames bent in place. There are two methods of framing a boat—one in which the frames are bent outside the ribbands and one in which they are bent inside the ribbands. The former is better wherever the frames can be bent to shape right on the boat, which includes almost all power boats and some sailboats where the frame is not too heavy. By bending the frames outside the ribbands, a light band of ⅛″ iron or about ¼″ oak can be clamped on each end of the frame, where the hard bend occurs, before bending, and just as the frame is pulled from the steam box. This helps prevent the frame from breaking or slivering. Another advantage is that the bilge stringers and even shelf and clamp can be used as ribbands, and when the boat is framed these members are already in place. If this method is used the thickness of ribbands and frames must be deducted. The lower ribband is generally placed on the outside, and the mold is as shown in Fig. 40.

Heavy sailboat frames with a reverse curve at the keel, as would be the case in Fig. 37, are bent to shape on the floor by use of a tackle and then placed in the boat. In this case the mold is made to the outside of the frame.

Molds are almost always placed at each station, and for smaller, light-framed boats are of about 1 1/16″ or 1¼″ lumber and for heavier craft 1½″ to 1¾″ stock. Each piece is pressed against nail or tack heads on the floor to obtain its shape, the same as in making patterns. One side is sawed to shape and the other piece or pieces marked off from it. One side is then fastened together to conform with the station line on the floor. The sheer line is marked or the top cut off to the bottom of the shelf (Fig. 40) and the bottom cut to the centerline. It is then turned over and the other half assembled on top of it.

Before fastening the two halves together, the height above base and distance out (from centerline) of the sheer line is marked on the opposite side of centerline on the loft floor, and this accurately locates the position of this half of the form. Both halves are tacked in place, a cross band is placed on the top, and a piece is fastened across the bottom to tie it securely together here; the centerline is marked on both cross band and bottom before removing the form from the floor.

Where the frames are to be bent outside the ribbands, as in Fig. 40, the shelf is generally placed on top of the forms before framing. In this case a beam pattern must be made to obtain the proper angle at which to cut the top of the form. Fig. 29 shows how the shape of this pattern is obtained.

It is not necessary to bevel the forms to the ribbands; instead the forward ones are placed aft of the line and the aft ones on the forward side.

No molds are required in V-bottom construction, and of course patterns for stem, keel, etc., are the same as in the round-bottom boat. Laying down and framing this boat is covered in Chapter 5.

5/ THE V-BOTTOM BOAT

LAYING DOWN OR LOFTING this type of boat offers no special problems, and where there is no curve to the frames, as is often the case, there are just three fore and aft lines used in fairing up; these are rabbet, chine, and sheer. In any case diagonals are seldom used, and then only on the bottom. Waterlines will adequately fair up the topsides and one or two buttocks the bottom. Greater accuracy, however, is required than in laying out the round-bottom boat.

There are in general two types of V-bottom construction, one in which all frames are sawed and battens used on the seams or hull double planked and the other in which the sawed frames are more widely spaced and light bent frames placed between. The latter has some advantages in that it dispenses with seam battens, which form ledges against which water lodges; it also involves less labor but often requires the use of a steam box for bending the intermediate frames. There are also varied combinations of these types of construction.

Then there is the bent-frame V-bottom in which the chine is superimposed over the bent oak frames. This greatly reduces the lofting time and, the frames being much thinner, results in a little roomier boat. Figure 41 illustrates these constructions.

THE CHINE

Laying out the chine requires some explanation. Figure 42 shows how this is laid out on the floor so that the notch may be cut in the frames before erecting them.

Some trimming will be required later, but it is a difficult task to try and cut out for the entire chine after the boat is set up, especially so if the frames are, as is usually the case, made of hardwood.

51

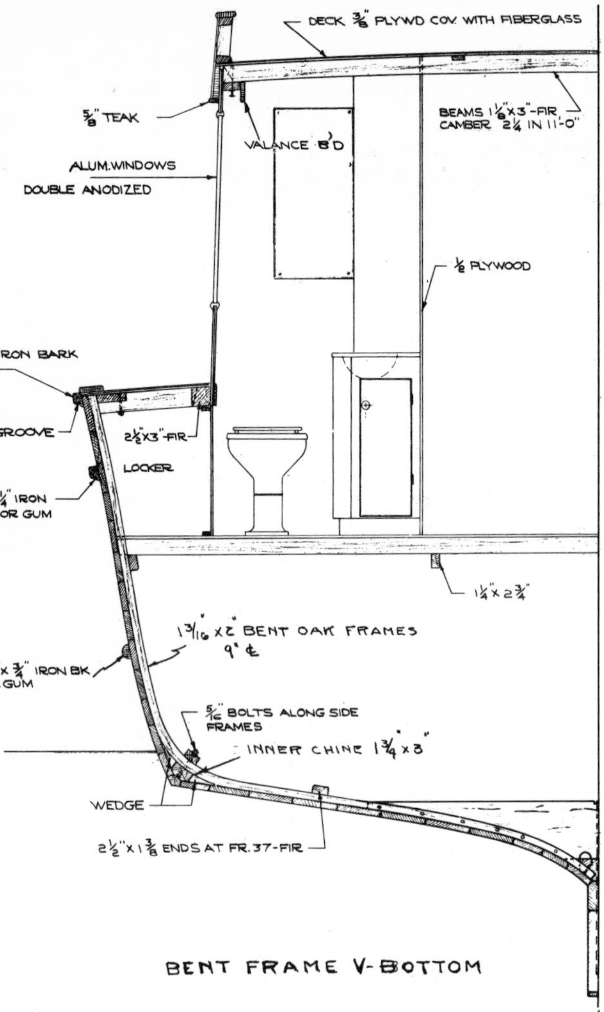
DECK 3/8" PLYWD COV. WITH FIBERGLASS
5/8" TEAK
VALANCE B'D
BEAMS 1 1/8"X3"-FIR
CAMBER 2 1/4 IN 11'-0"
ALUM.WINDOWS
DOUBLE ANODIZED
1/2 PLYWOOD
GUARD 7/8"X2" IRON BARK
OR GUM
DRIP GROOVE
2 1/2"X3"-FIR
LOCKER
1 3/8"X2 1/4" IRON
BARK OR GUM
1 1/4"X2 3/4"
1 3/16 X2" BENT OAK FRAMES
9" ℄
1 1/4"X 3/4" IRON BK
OR GUM
5/16" BOLTS ALONG SIDE
FRAMES
INNER CHINE 1 3/4 X 3"
WEDGE
2 1/2"X1 3/8 ENDS AT FR.37-FIR
BENT FRAME V-BOTTOM

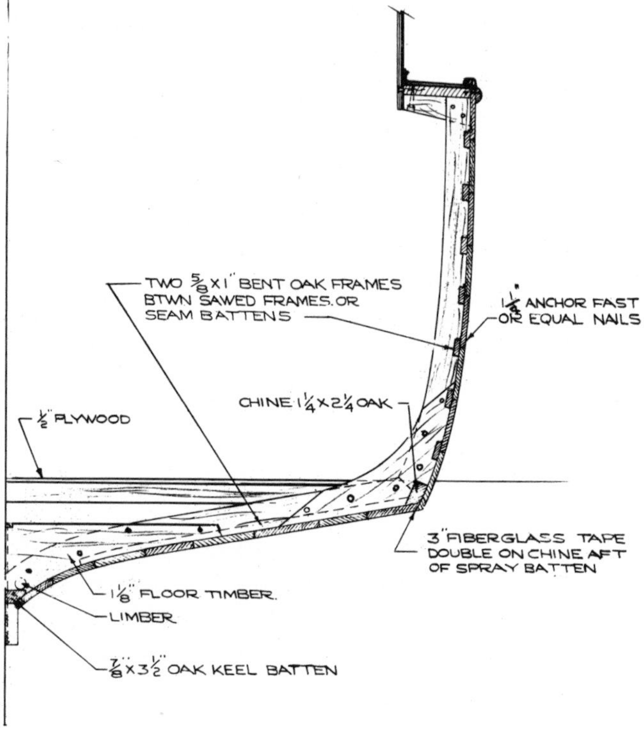
TWO 5/8X1" BENT OAK FRAMES
BTWN SAWED FRAMES.OR
SEAM BATTENS
1 1/4" ANCHOR FAST
OR EQUAL NAILS
CHINE 1 1/4X2 1/4 OAK
1/2" PLYWOOD
3" FIBERGLASS TAPE
DOUBLE ON CHINE AFT
OF SPRAY BATTEN
1 1/8" FLOOR TIMBER.
LIMBER
7/8X3 1/2" OAK KEEL BATTEN

FIG. 41. V-bottom cruiser:
(left) bent frame and (right) sawn frame

Sometimes there is no outer chine. The bottom planking overlaps the top plank and a chine batten is let into the frame for fastening purposes. While this is a labor saver it has little other virtue. (See Fig. 41.)

The chine may be made of one or two pieces. The two-piece chine, as in Fig. 42, is much easier to make, and if the two pieces are properly screw-fastened and glued together it is just as good a job as rabbeting it out of one piece. Run-abouts having no external keel usually have a keel batten which is laid out in a similar manner.

In laying out for the chine the angle is bisected by measuring the spots Y and Z equidistant from the chine corner; from these intersect equal arcs and draw the line D-E. Mark off the plank thickness (if not already done) and the width of the outer chine. The inner face can then be laid out as shown. Square off line D-E. The inner chine can then be laid out. The outer one will of course vary in thickness, being thinner forward, and the inner one can also be tapered forward for ease in bending.

FRAME BEVELS

Figure 43 shows how bevels are obtained for each frame. Where these are spaced more than twenty-four inches apart a light "square" may be tacked to-gether and the distance between frames marked on it. The square is stood up "square off" the frame line with the corner on the line; the straight-edge is held with lower end on the next frame and intersecting the square at the same height

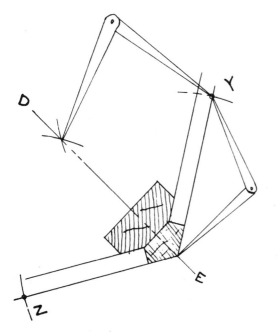

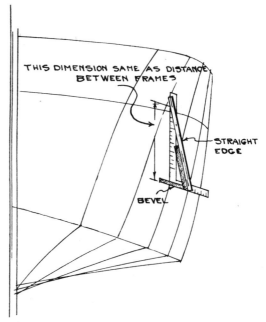

FIG. 42. Laying out V-bottom chine   **FIG. 43.** V-bottom boat: frame bevels

Photo by Ray Krantz

FIG. 44. V-bottom hull with combination of sawn and bent frames

above floor as the frames are inches apart and the bevel taken as shown. This bevel can then be marked on a board or applied directly to the frame.

A more exact method is to make a beveling stick as shown in Fig. 45. The distance A is two frame spacings or twice the distance between frames, and the stick is applied like a rule, measuring across three frames to obtain the bevel of the middle one. In Fig. 20 the distance between frames 1 and 3 and square off station 2 will give the bevel at any point on station 2. When beveling the pieces do not make the common mistake of beveling both pieces for the same side of the boat.

ASSEMBLING THE FRAME

The lines are transferred from the floor to the lumber in the same manner as for the molds in Chapter 2. One side only is marked and cut to shape, and these pieces are used as a pattern for laying out the other side.

In assembling the frames it must be kept in mind that the line on the floor represents the joining surfaces of the members—the shape of the upper surface of the lower pieces and the under surface of the upper ones. In Fig. 46 the latter would be the floor and gusset. The lower pieces are therefore under bevel and the upper ones standing bevel. A small square is used to square up the frame line on the floor to the edge of the frame (Fig. 47). The bottom pieces are thus correctly placed and tacked down. A cross band is placed on each frame, generally at the sheer, and centerline marked on it and on the floor of the

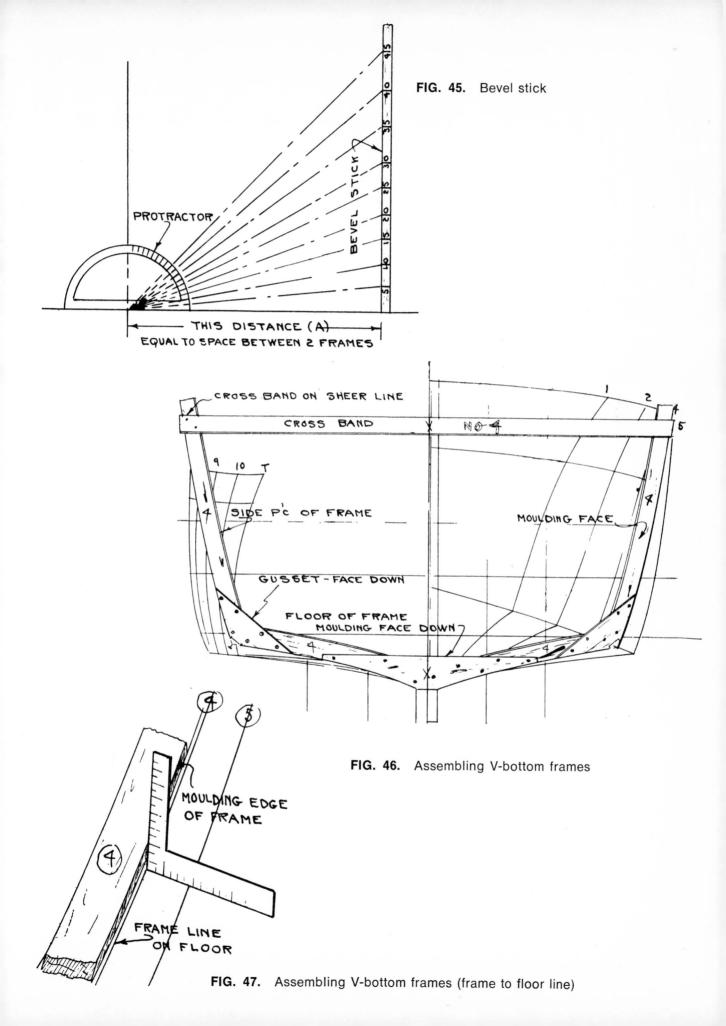

FIG. 45. Bevel stick

PROTRACTOR

BEVEL STICK

THIS DISTANCE (A)
EQUAL TO SPACE BETWEEN 2 FRAMES

CROSS BAND ON SHEER LINE

CROSS BAND   NO 4

SIDE P'C OF FRAME

MOULDING FACE

GUSSET—FACE DOWN

FLOOR OF FRAME
MOULDING FACE DOWN

FIG. 46. Assembling V-bottom frames

MOULDING EDGE
OF FRAME

FRAME LINE
ON FLOOR

FIG. 47. Assembling V-bottom frames (frame to floor line)

frame. The same method used in assembling the forms, Chapter 4, is used here for the frames, except that the chine corner, as well as the sheer, is located on the opposite side of centerline on the floor to aid in placing correctly this side of the frame.

Waterproof glue between all joining surfaces, frame to gusset, etc., will add immensely to the strength of the frame, and either bolts or screws are used to fasten them together.

SETTING UP THE BOAT

The boat is set up in the same manner as was the round bottom, except that the sawed frames take the place of the forms, and the molded surface or joint between floor and frame will come on the frame mark on the keel. Here as in Fig. 48 the entire frame must be trued up square and plumb and well braced and the floor piece bolted or permanently fastened to the keel.

The chine is next. A small piece the same shape as the chine and a small batten are handy in fairing up and trimming the notches before bending the chine piece. Fit the chine to stem, and, starting here, bend it in aft. Fastenings should be into the gussets rather than the ends of the frame pieces, and screws are generally used. With a two-piece chine the inner piece had best be faired off to the frames before the outer one is put on.

The boat builder often fits in all the seam battens if used before planking, but the amateur had best put them on one at a time as he planks the boat.

Small boats such as runabouts and sometimes fairly large cruisers are generally set up upside down. This greatly facilitates much of the work, particularly planking the bottom.

Figures 49 and 50 illustrate this procedure, the former generally for small craft. The set-up line is marked on each frame and the cross band nailed or screw-fastened to it and position of set-up stringers marked on cross band and

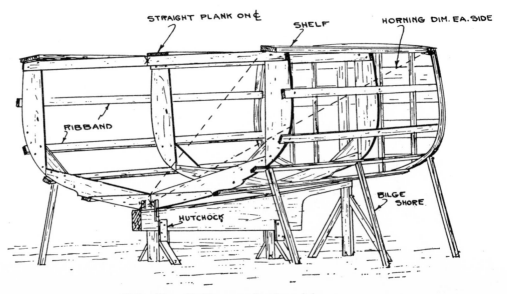

FIG. 48. Setting up keel and forms

centerline. The stringers are so located as to clear the forward frames as shown.

Figure 50 shows the frames set up on the shelf. The latter must, of course, be so supported as to take the same fore and aft slope or sheer as when afloat.

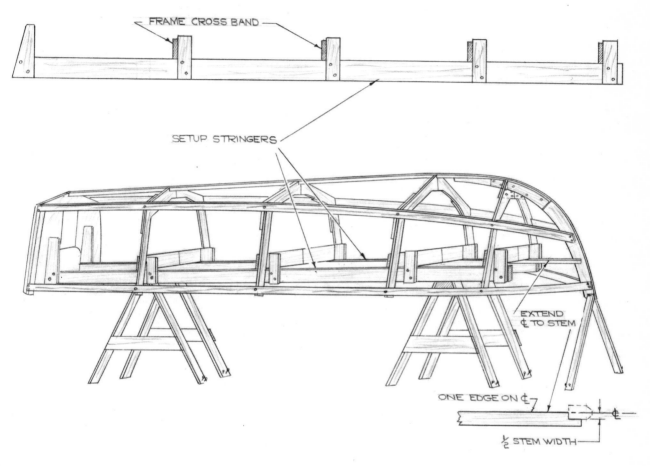

FIG. 49. Boat set up on setup stringers

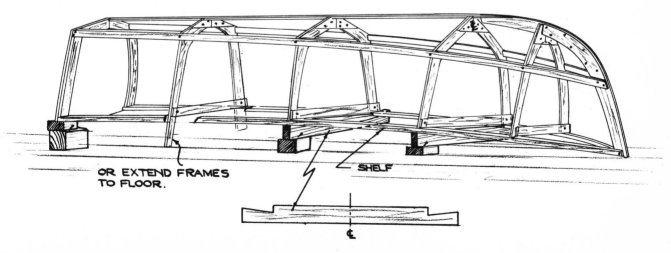

FIG. 50. Frames set on shelf upside down

The straight sheered hull offers no problem. The curved or sprung sheer is a bit more difficult, and measurements must be taken at each frame to the floor, if straight and level, or to a chalkline.

Sometimes the frame ends are left long to extend to the floor and the shelf, if any, put on after the boat is right side up.

Turning a heavy boat right side up is sometimes a problem. Often this is done after the bottom only is planked to eliminate a considerable portion of the weight.

PLANKING AND SEAM BATTENS

Generally no attempt is made to run all the bottom planks to the stem, and they are run in to the best advantage with the upper ones ending on and screw-fastened to the chine. Seam battens are usually screw-fastened through the plank into the battens and sometimes clinch-nailed from the outside. Caulking is often dispensed with, especially so in light work, and a waterproof glue, seam batten compound, or double plank cement placed on the batten makes the job watertight.

Where softwood frames are used, planking should be screw-fastened. The light bent frames are often bent in after the boat is planked; plank fastenings can be drilled from inside using a thin batten to mark each frame for drilling before bending frame. Sometimes they are screw-fastened from inside and glued to planking.

Double planking is often used; the first layer may be diagonal. Seam battens, except perhaps one wide one in the middle of bottom, can then usually be dispensed with. Muslin is sometimes placed between the layers laid in glue or paint, but a tight job can be had without this. The inner layer is thinnest and is fastened from the inside to the outer planking with one or more rows of screws between each frame, the number depending on the distance between frames. The screws had best be placed to come near each edge of each outer plank, by drilling the holes through inner plank from outside about an inch above each strake of outer planking. As the strakes are put on, the screws can thus be accurately located. Double planking the bottom with both layers diagonal results in a very strong job and uses short lengths. Topsides are sometimes so treated, and both layers may be laid fore and aft on the entire hull.

6/ ASSEMBLING FRAME AND SETTING UP BOAT

ASSUMING THE PATTERNS AND FORMS ARE ALL MADE, we are now ready to start actual construction of the boat. Starting with the stem, be sure the aft side is square and straight. Laying the pattern on the stick, mark rabbet, bearding line, and shape of face. The rabbet and bearding line are marked through the pattern by drilling small holes through it, driving in finish nails, and then springing a batten through these spots.

FIG. 51. Keel and horn timber of motor sailer   *Photo by Ray Krantz*

CUTTING THE RABBET

In cutting the rabbet, use as a template a short piece the same thickness as the planking as shown in Fig. 52, with the end sawed square. This template represents the planking. A spot is trimmed every eight inches or so, fitting the piece down until the upper edge is flush with the rabbet and the lower to the bearding line. Trim out between the spots and leave an inch or so of wood at the top, next to the sheer line, and five or six inches at the lower end. The width of the stem face is next gauged off and the stem sides beveled off from the rabbet to the stem face. If this is a conventional sailboat, the same process is followed for forefoot, keel, and horn timber. Where these are also shaped on each side, as is the case with a wide keel tapered at each end to the narrower stem and rudder width, the pieces are all tapered and shaped first and the rabbet cut afterward. It is not necessary that the various members fair into one another inside or above the rabbet line; that is, the horn timber may be an inch narrower each side than the shaft log, and no attention is paid to fairing the sides into one another, in this case above the rabbet line.

The power boat's keel, as in Fig. 35, is sawed to shape and planed smooth and square. The rabbet forward is cut in the same manner as the stem; along the top of the keel the depth and width are laid out as in Fig. 36.

STEM AND FOREFOOT

Where a forefoot knee is used, it is usually specified natural crook hackmatack or fir. These are often hard to obtain, and as they sometimes contain considerable sap wood they are liable to dry rot. A straight-grain piece cut with a little more depth will serve very well. In bolting up stem and knee, the stem face is generally too narrow for the bolt head, and to remedy this the bolt edges can be sawed or ground off, forming a narrow head as in Fig. 52. After bolting up, a thin batten is bent along the rabbet and bearding lines where stem, knee and keel join, and this portion is finished.

The joining surfaces of all backbone members should be glued together. It is really handier to glue up the entire assembly and bolt it afterward.

SHAFT LOG AND STERN POST

We can next turn our attention to the aft end. Shaft logs are generally in two pieces, upper and lower, though the former may also form the horn timber. They are sometimes splined as in Fig. 53; however, if carefully fitted and glued together and well bolted, a plain joint without splines will not cause trouble, provided the stuffing box is on the inside and not the outer end of the log.

Many plans show a hardwood stern post bolted to the aft end of keel and

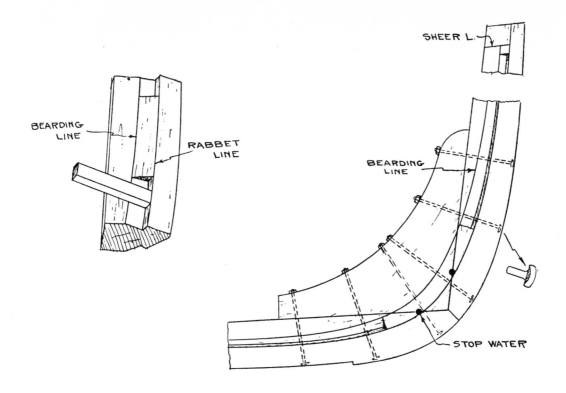

FIG. 52. Stern rabbet

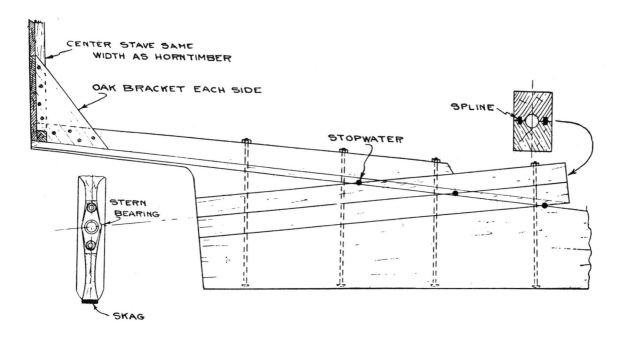

FIG. 53. Shaft log and horn timber

shaft log and also tenoned top and bottom. This member has always seemed to me to serve no essential purpose except in large vessels, and on the West Coast of the United States it is seldom used. Its only purpose would be to bolt the stern bearing to, and longer lag screws into the shaft log end will do this almost as well. Another disadvantage, in a sailboat, is that the stern post swells, forcing the rudder aft and jambing it in the rudder tube above. Stern bearings can also be pocket-bolted, as in Fig. 54.

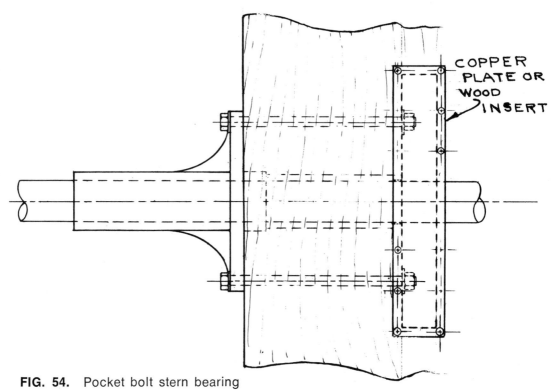

FIG. 54. Pocket bolt stern bearing

The two-bolt stern bearing has some advantages for pleasure boats where a large heavy wheel is not required; the end of the log and keel can then be fined away nicely, allowing a good flow of water to the wheel. The stern bearing should be on hand so that this can be done before the boat is set up, and the shaft log bolts should be kept six or eight inches forward of the end to allow for trimming. One sees many boats on drydock with almost the full width of keel squarely in front of a small propeller. The owner is paying for this every mile he runs, besides the vibration caused when each blade crosses this flat spot.

Stopwaters of some dry softwood should be placed at each crossing of rabbet and joint. These are generally about ½″ in diameter and larger for larger boats. The hole is first drilled through with the worm following the joint, and the tight-fitting stopwater, which is merely a plug, is driven through and sawed off at each end.

THE KEELSON

Most heavy cruisers and work boats, also some lighter boats, have keelsons (Fig. 55). This makes for a stronger but somewhat heavier backbone and provides a splendid fastening for the frame ends, also a back-up for the garboard plank and garboard seam.

It should be laid out on the mold loft floor; you have the width of it and the depth. This is laid out at each station on top of the keel on loft floor. The

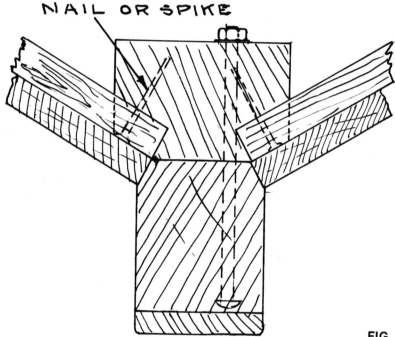

FIG. 55. Keelson detail

stations are marked off on the keelson timber. At each station the distance down from the top, or up from bottom, also width at top of keel is marked and a batten sprung between points. The surplus wood is trimmed off and the pockets for the frames laid out. Use a frame end, fitting it in each pocket, making it a bit loose, as the frame is bound to swell a little in the steam box.

BOLTING UP THE BACKBONE

The entire backbone is bolted together while lying flat on some horses, and if the frames, as in most sailboats, are to be let into the keel and deadwood, this is provided for now. If possible it is best to bolt on the iron keel, but this cannot always be done. Some builders put the bolts in with the top ends sticking through the wood keel and then by locating the bolt holes in the floor timbers drill the holes through them. Where the bolts are set up on top of the keel, as in Fig. 39, it is a simple matter to bolt on the casting while the whole assembly is lying on its side. Heavy ship felt is usually placed between casting and wood and the upper part of casting painted with red lead and wood keel with copper paint. Where a lead keel is used, holes can be drilled through floors, wood keel, and casting in one operation.

Dry, warm weather plays havoc with joints and opens up large checks in the backbone structure, but below water it cannot be painted with oil paint, as this prevents copper paint from sticking later on. Kerosene is one remedy for this, and special anti-check preparations are available.

SETTING UP THE BOAT

Now to set up the boat. Figure 40 shows a cross-section about midships of a power boat with keel resting on the keel block or post and one of the forms in place. The keel posts are first set up, one at each end of the straight part of the keel, and from the loft floor the rake or slope of the keel is obtained and the blocks cut off at the correct height and slope to place the waterlines level and stations perpendicular. A chalkline may be stretched between these two and the other posts cut accordingly. A chalkline is also used alongside to line them up fore and aft.

Do not make the mistake of setting the boat up too close to the floor, as it makes hard work of planking the bottom. On the average cruiser the keel rabbet at the lowest point should not be much less than thirty-eight inches from the floor, as a man can then squat on his haunches almost any place under the boat.

There will be some scrap pieces left over from keel and deadwood, and as these are the same width as keel (generally) they will make ideal keel blocks; brace them and fasten well to the floor and set the keel on top. On each side is fastened a hutchock as shown and a tall post placed forward and aft under the stem and horn timber. It is important that the keel, stem, and entire backbone be set up perfectly plumb. Use a level on the side of the keel and the power boat's stem. A plumb bob is dropped down from the end of the long overhanging stem and horn timber of a sailboat to a chalkline stretched alongside the keel blocks below to plumb up these ends. The ends must be securely shored and braced, and keep the braces as much out of the way as possible. A stem can often be braced from the top to the side of a building.

We are now ready to set up the first form, or with the wide transom boat the transom may be first; if so, set it up at the proper rake, and, using a batten or steel tape, horn each side to a spot on the center of the keel as shown in Fig. 48. The transom or form must be adjusted so that the horning distances on each side are exactly equal, which squares it up with the centerline of the boat. Place a brace aft on each side to hold the horning position and a shore on each bilge.

TRUEING UP THE FRAME

All forms are plumbed fore and aft as well as thwartships, and by measuring on each side to the form that was set up first and horned, they are kept square with the ship. Each form is cleated or toenailed to the keel (Fig. 48) and tied together on top with a temporary tie lath on each side on top of the cross bands. Also a temporary shore is placed each side to be shifted later to the ribbands.

An excellent method for tying the whole together where its use is feasible is to place a long straight-edged plank down the center of the cross bands as in Figs. 40 and 48. A piece of wide planking will do, and if the nails are carefully pulled and the holes plugged, no damage to plank will result.

The procedure will vary with the type of boat, but the object of course is to erect the backbone and temporary forms around which the boat will be built plumb and square with the world and to secure them firmly in place. A little extra effort and time expended in doing so will be well worth while and will prevent much grief later on.

Transoms must be kneed to the horn timber by either a hardwood or a plywood piece each side, as in Fig. 53, or by a knee on top of the horn timber.

RIBBANDS

Ribbands will come next; however, if the boat has a sawed shelf as in Fig. 40, it is best to place this first, as it securely braces the whole structure against the strain of bending the ribbands. The shape of this member may be obtained from the mold loft floor, or directly from the boat by placing the boards on top of the forms. The loft floor is really the most workmanlike, and the pieces can be beveled and all scarfed and fastened together before putting them in place.

There is always some fore and aft slope to the sheer, so take the distance between stations on this slope and transfer it to the shelf; otherwise these distances will be short.

The location of the frames can also be marked. In some cases the frames are let in flush with the edge of the shelf, which makes an excellent fastening for the guard.

Ribband sizes and their number will depend on the size and shape of the boat and should be closely spaced at the bilge where the hard bend comes, and if the frame is bent outside, the corners of these ribbands should be flattened off to avoid kinks. The average cruiser requires a ribband of about $1\frac{5}{8}''$ x $2\frac{1}{2}''$ and small lighter boats as small as $1\frac{1}{16}''$ x $1\frac{3}{4}''$. Bilge stringers, where they serve also as ribbands, as in Fig. 40, should have their inner corners chamfered. Taper the forward ends for ease in bending and to form a fair curve, and of course both ends in case of a double ender.

The ribbands should be placed on the boat in pairs, one on one side and then its mate on the other, to even up the pressure against the forms. Fasten the forward ends at the stem first and bend them in against the forms. It may be necessary to steam at least some of them where there is quite a twist or hard bend. Long screws set up over washers are best for fastening, though wire nails are often used. The double-head nail, if obtainable, is of some advantage in disassembling later.

With the boat all ribbanded up, the bilge shores can be shifted to the ribbands and the temporary stay laths removed and other braces shifted to be as much out of the way as possible.

7/ FRAMING AND PLANKING

BENT OAK FRAMES, where not too large, are bent hot right on the boat. A frame about two inches square is about as large as can be bent in this manner. The stiffness of the oak will have a great deal to do with its ease of bending. Heavier frames, especially those for sailboats, should be bent on the shop floor and then placed in the boat.

Figure 40 shows the typical light frame of the average power cruiser. Each piece is grabbed hot from the steam box and where the bend is hard a band quickly clamped on. The lower end is placed on the keel and a man inside quickly cuts the underside with a chisel to fit on top of the keel, assuming there is no keelson. It is then bent up against the ribbands and clamped in place. Two men work outside, one of them bending the frame and clamping the top end, the other at the bilge taking care of this part. The frame can be tapped up or down to suit and a nail driven into the keel to secure it here. The frame is nailed to each ribband with bright (not galvanized) wire nails. Some builders toenail frames into ribbands on the side, and where frames are bent inside they are nailed from outside through the ribband. Each frame should be pulled up tight against the ribbands on both its edges, and where there is a tendency to pull off, a clamp may be left on until the frame sets. A large number of clamps is an advantage and about five the minimum. Before framing is started the location of each frame should be marked on the ribbands, with particular attention paid to bulkhead frames to get them straight and fair. When there is trouble pulling them out to the ribbands, when bent inside, tapping them down on top will help.

Where there is excessive flare forward longer frames than required are used, and the top end is pulled well out and stay lathed in this position and left until the frame takes a permanent set.

A word of precaution: These frames tend to push the shelf up, forming a hump in the shear, so brace the shelf down from on top or use other means to prevent this.

67

Heavy frames are bent on the floor by the aid of a block and tackle. Cleats are fastened to the floor much as the cleats on the transom mold, Fig. 25, and to form a bend a little greater than required on the boat. A band is clamped on as before, and as the frame is bent around it is wedged against the cleats. A few dogs to wedge against are very handy. If there is a reverse curve in the heel, this is also bent in; a stay lath is then quickly nailed across the frame to hold it in shape, and it is fitted into the boat and pulled tightly against the ribbands while still hot. The floor cleats must be close together, and a solid piece with the curve sawed in it at the hardest part of the bend is less likely to cause breakage than the cleats. There are several excellent arrangements and devices for bending frames, one in which the lines to the block and tackle are so arranged that the reverse curve as well as the main curve is pulled in at the same time. A stubborn bend on the frame heel can be pulled out, as illustrated in Fig. 56.

Frame material must not be too dry. Most boat shops make a practice of soaking the frames two or three days before bending. Covering the pile with sacks and frequently wetting them down will help. Where a frame breaks square off in bending it is a sign of poor oak. Long slivers in a few of the frames, if tacked in place with copper tacks, are generally permissible. All oak is bent with the layers or grain parallel to the bend, as shown in Fig. 40. Frames must be hot and steamed thoroughly through and through. It does not take long with good live steam to do this, the length of time depending on the size of the piece. Twenty minutes is ample for a small light frame. If it comes from the box limber and too hot to hold, it is ready to bend. One can always try a frame, and if something tells you it isn't going to make the bend, put it back in the box. Bend the longer frames first, as some of the cripples can be worked in forward where the frame is shorter and the bend not severe.

Bulkhead frames forward or aft where there is much bevel should be beveled on the side against which the bulkhead will fit. This can be done before the frame is bent by obtaining the bevels from the ribbands with the aid of a straightedge across to the other side. A less efficient method is to bend in the frame first, bevel a few spots, remove the frame and trim the bevels, and it can be replaced without steaming.

A very heavy frame can be laminated using two pieces. This requires quite a large number of clamps. After bending in place, time is allowed for them to dry; the outer piece is then removed and a very liberal amount of glue applied before clamping together again. It is important that no voids occur between the laminations, as these are an invitation to dry rot.

THE SAWED FRAME

In building sailboats it is often necessary to saw to shape a few of the frames next the transom. The shape of these can be obtained from the mold loft or by making a pattern directly from the ribbands. Sawed frames are also used in

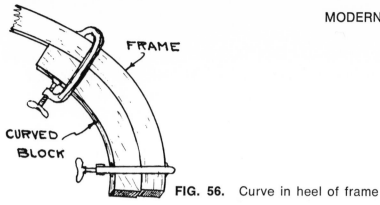

FIG. 56. Curve in heel of frame

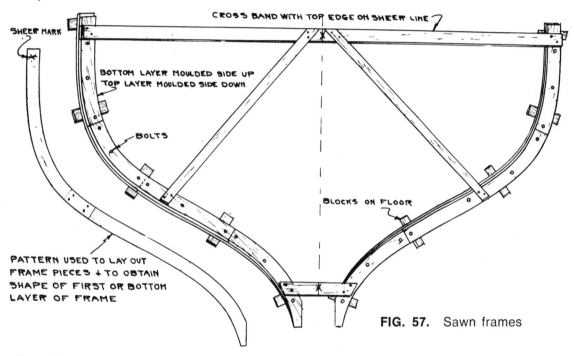

FIG. 57. Sawn frames

lieu of molds; these are made in two layers with the butts well separated. Bevels are obtained by use of a bevel stick, as described in Chapter 5, and put together with bolts much in the same manner as a V-bottom frame as shown in Fig. 57. A pattern is first made of the frame shape, and from it the various pieces are marked off. Don't forget that one layer is always under and the other standing bevel, also that each layer must be half for one side and half for the other side of the boat.

To assemble the frame, lay some blocks on the floor, roughly to the shape of the frame, and spread out one layer on it, face or molded side up. With the aid of the pattern these can be fitted together, and by measuring across the top at the sheer height the correct width is obtained, as was done in assembling the V-bottom frame. This layer is now tacked in place, the upper layer placed face down over it, and the two bolted together. The object of the blocks is to prevent drilling into the floor for the bolts. Waterproof glue between will add immensely to the strength of the frame.

Sawed frames can also be assembled directly from the loft floor by putting the under bevel pieces down first and squaring the line up from the floor, as shown in Fig. 47 and described in Chapter 5. The shape of the opposite side of the frame is marked on the floor from the pattern. The layers are in this case screw-fastened together.

The sawed frame is rather difficult for the amateur to tackle, and comparatively few of the professional builders are familiar with this construction. The frames, being rather fragile, must be well braced before removing them from the floor; besides the cross band, an X brace is also used to hold them in shape.

Large, heavily constructed wooden craft have all their frames sawed to shape, but this larger construction should be classified as ship-building rather than boat-building.

FLOOR TIMBERS

With the frames all in place, the next step will be the floors. These are usually laid out as in Fig. 58 by placing a board across the keel and marking the frames on it. As one function of the floors is to tie the hull proper to the keel, they must be securely bolted to the latter. Through bolts with nuts on top are best, though where the keel is quite deep a drift bolt is satisfactory. Where floors are placed alongside they should be fitted tightly against the frames. Carriage bolts

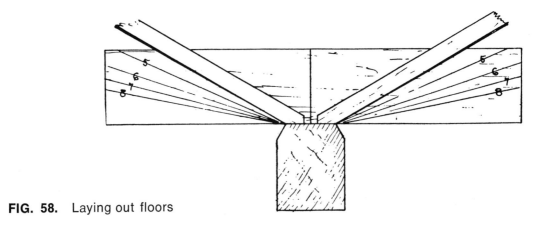

FIG. 58. Laying out floors

are best in bolting frames to the floors. In light construction galvanized nails driven through the floors into the oak frames are quite permissible; the square boat nail is best. When floors are placed on top of the frames, at least one bolt should be placed at the ends of the floors through the frame. Do not forget to provide adequate limbers for the passage of bilge water through the floors.

Floors must fit tightly against frames, and floors at forward end should be placed on forward side of frames for ease of fitting.

Planking is generally the next step, though in many instances, particularly with sailboats where lodge knees must be fitted, the deck frame is put in first.

It is also often easier to put in the bulkheads before planking, removing the temporary ribbons if frames are bent outside.

PLANKING

The general procedure in planking is to start with the sheer strake and plank down to the bilge and then start with the garboard and put the last plank or shutter in on the round of the bilge where the plank will be wider on the outside face.

The first step is to run a batten on the upper bilge. The widest or deepest spot on the top side of hull is first ascertained and the plank widths laid off here and batten placed on the lower edge of the lowest strake. Allow it to take a natural shape or curve without edge set or bend; this line will run pretty well up on the stem. The sheer line is run in with the batten to the sheer marks on the molds, though of course if the shelf is already in place this will not be necessary.

The space at transom and stem is then divided up to accommodate the number of strakes. To eliminate edge set as much as possible where there is considerable flare, the sheer strake may be tapered at stem to just width enough for a fastening in the nib. Where the frames are notched into the shelf and top of beams flush with top of shelf, the top strakes need not run to the stem but take their natural shape and run out to a shim edge where they can be well fastened to the shelf; the shim points are covered by the guard.

With the plank widths obtained at ends and midships, the widths are obtained at intermediate stations spaced every four or five feet. The "liner," as the planking layout man is called, makes a plank scale as shown in Fig. 59. By

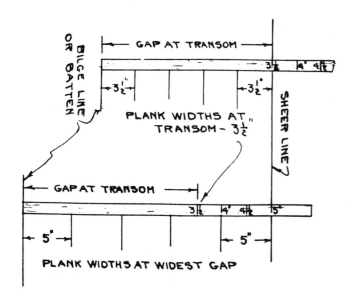

FIG. 59. Planking scale

measuring with this at any intermediate point the exact plank width is obtained. As in the illustration, the widest girth is marked on each side of the scale and on one side the forward width at stem and the other the aft width at transom. The space between is divided to represent inches in the difference between the widest part of the plank and the end. The scale placed at any point between the sheer and bilge line will give the width of the plank in inches at this point. Another method is to space the planking on a batten at the widest girth, and by holding this diagonally across at different points the plank widths may be measured square off the sheer line.

If the wedged seam is used there is little point in shaping or spiling the planks to present even widths, and the only shaping required is to alleviate the edge set of the planks, letting the ends run where they will, at least on the topsides.

Transom planking is almost never caulked, generally double; the outer layer is fitted edge to edge and glued. If painted, it may be wedged. Hull planking should overlap the transom plank and not vice versa.

BEVELING THE PLANKS

After the first strake is on, the subsequent ones must be beveled to provide a caulking seam. A small pocket bevel is used for this purpose. The boat builder buys the standard twelve-inch bevel and cuts off the short end; the underside of this is filed as shown in Fig. 3 to represent the seam, or to a taper of $\frac{1}{16}''$ in $1''$, which is the standard seam. For wedged seams, however, it is 10 degrees. A bevel board from two to three feet long is made with which to space off the spots at which the bevel is to be taken. These are numbered 1, 2, 3, etc., along the strake, the bevel at each spot marked on the board and then transferred to

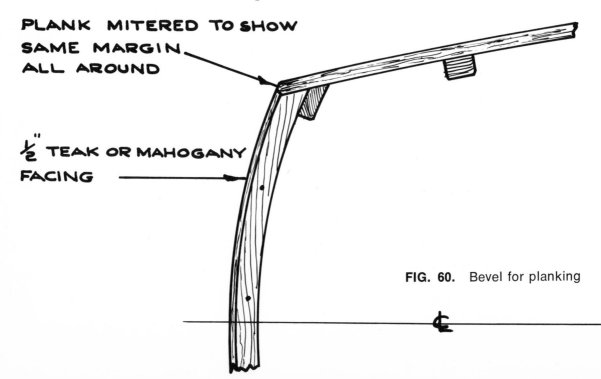

PLANK MITERED TO SHOW
SAME MARGIN
ALL AROUND

$\frac{1}{2}''$ TEAK OR MAHOGANY
FACING

FIG. 60. Bevel for planking

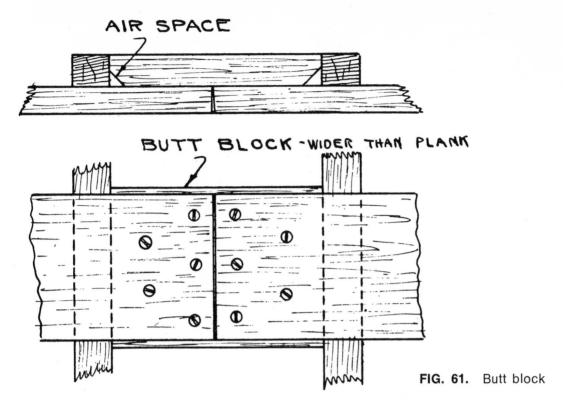

FIG. 61. Butt block

the plank. Plane each spot to the correct bevel and then with a hand jointer plane fair up between the spots. The wedged seam is covered in Chapter 8. You may have to make your own bevel (see Chapter 1).

PUTTING THEM ON THE BOAT

Where there is much bend the plank will require steaming. The garboard or strake next the keel, which has quite a twist, is almost always steamed. The sheer strake is put on first and the boat is planked down from this. Where they can be used, a few door clamps are excellent for pulling the planks tight, edge to edge. When these cannot be used, planking dogs are handiest. These can be purchased at a marine supply house at small cost. Where these are not available, a block can be clamped to the frame and the plank wedged against it. A stout clamp must be used, however, and tightly set up, or the wedging will soon twist the clamp out of shape. Boat clamps are of course indispensable for pulling the plank tightly to the frame.

Even with the most careful lining, lumps are bound to appear on the strake's edge, especially at the butts. These must be taken off and the strake's edge kept in a nice fair line. A rabbet plane is most useful for this purpose. Fair up the plank edge with a light batten and plane down to it. A strip tacked on the bottom of a wooden rabbet plane narrowing the exposed blade to the plank thickness will make the plane much easier to handle on the strake's edge.

FIG. 62. (Opposite, above) Planking a 42-foot troller

FIG. 63. (Opposite, below) Boat set up upside down. Note hollowed block under clamp to pull down plank edges.

Photo by Ray Krantz

FIG. 64. (Above) Double-end motor sailer planked down to bilge. Stern post nicely faired in above and below stern bearing.

Photo by Ray Krantz

Butts are best made on hardwood butt blocks placed between the frames, except where the frames are quite wide, or on the bottom where floor and frame together form a wide landing, and again with wedged seams they are often omitted. Figure 61 shows a properly fitted butt block with the inside corners taken off to allow for ventilation and the passage of any water that may run down the inside of the boat. Plank butts are always screw-fastened.

When the planking is finished down to the turn of the bilge, operations are transferred and the boat is planked up from the keel. The molds are often removed at this point, first placing a stay lath across the boat at each mold. An intermediate brace across the ship lower down is also sometimes advisable to preserve the shape of the boat. The bottom plank widths are then laid out at the widest space or gap and a batten run in to represent the upper edge of the garboard. It is very important to run the forward end of this plank up as high as possible on the stem, and often a wider plank is used in order to accomplish this. For instance, a twelve-inch plank is ordered for a garboard that is ten inches wide or less amidships. The purpose of running the line up on the stem is to avoid as much as possible the edge set which is sure to develop in the next two or three strakes.

THE GARBOARD

Figure 65 shows how a garboard is laid out. The wide batten is allowed to take its natural shape, and except perhaps at the very forward end the top edge will represent the upper edge of the garboard. A pair of dividers is used to mark on the batten the width of the plank at each frame; a pitch mark is placed on batten and keel and later transferred to the plank to locate accurately the fore and aft position of the plank when fitting it in place. Where the plank is fairly thick, strips are tacked onto the frames to furr the batten out so that its face represents the face of the garboard, and widths are taken to the outer edge of the rabbet. Sometimes a pattern is made the exact shape of the forward end; it need be but four or five feet long.

FIG. 65. Garboard layout

There being considerable twist forward, steaming is almost always required. Shore and clamp it in place, and if, as is often the case, it does not fit exactly here and there, it can be allowed to cool and take its shape, after which it may be removed and refitted.

The scaling batten cannot be made much use of on the bottom. Keep the widths at the transom such as to avoid edge set and, forward, run the first few strakes up high enough to accomplish the same purpose. Look ahead, however, and lay the ends, or nibs, out tentatively so that the last two or three will not run out to narrow shim points.

It may be necessary to spile or shape some of the planks, especially at the forward end, wherever the edge set is too great to bend them. A spiling batten is used for this purpose. This is a fairly wide batten first tacked on where the plank will go and allowed to take its natural shape. Upon this is measured the distance from one edge at numerous points to the edge of the preceding strake, much as the garboard was laid out. When removed and laid on the plank, the measurements will give the required shape without edge setting. Some edge set is of course permissible, and the original plank need not be quite the width required to accommodate all the spiling shown by the batten.

STEALERS

In some boats a stealer plank or two will be required. The forty-two-foot troller shown in Fig. 62 is one example. This is used at a lower part of hull aft to eliminate heavy edge set, where this cannot be accomplished by fishtailing the strake because the width required is too great.

The single strake is butted on a frame in this instance, and two planks take its place, extending aft to the stern or stern rabbet. Both are fishtailed and all the edge set eliminated, at least for the next strake.

In the V-bottom boat all the bottom strakes need not run to the stem. They may end on the chine. In this case it is best, though not essential, to nib or jog one plank into the next in order to avoid shim ends. Fasten to the chine with screws.

DOUBLE PLANKING

There are at least three methods. In one, a light diagonal forms the inner layer and a heavier fore and aft strake the outer planking. Another has both layers running fore and aft, and this is the easiest to apply, as clamps can be used on both layers. The third has both layers diagonal, generally the same thickness and running in opposite directions; often the bottom only is diagonaled and used only on V-bottom hulls.

Double plank cement, Thiokol, or sometimes waterproof glue is used between the layers. It is very important that sufficient cement or glue be used to fill all voids on account of the dry-rot hazard. Double plank cement can be obtained containing a fungicide, and this of course is very desirable.

In any case, the inner layer is merely tacked in place, using bronze or copper nails placed near the frame edges to clear the through fastenings later.

A little ingenuity can save much labor. For instance, when both layers are fore and aft, the inner layer is screw-fastened to the outer one from inside, a screw being placed at upper and lower edges of the outer plank and about an inch or less from the edge, one row between each bent oak frame; drill the lower screw holes from the outside before the next outer plank is put on. A similar procedure can be used for the other two methods.

The outer layer is of course fastened through both layers into the frame.

PLANK FASTENINGS

Plank fastenings may be either nails, screws, or rivets. The former hold very well; anyone who has seen a plank repair job on the ways will realize this. The nails hold so tightly in the oak frame that they generally pull through the plank and remain sticking in the frame. In heavy plank and for the best job, the topsides are generally bunged or plugged with deck plugs. Often, however, they are merely countersunk, and though this is not always done, it is good practice to first break the skin of the plank with a belt punch to leave a clean hole. Set the nails sufficiently to hold the seam composition about ⅛″. The setting is done after the boat is planked. One man holds against the frame with a heavy hold-on or a maul head while the other sets the nails. This is advisable at least with bent oak frames.

Screw-fastening is of course excellent, especially if the screws are of Everdure or other alloy made especially for the purpose. Where the frames are of spruce or other soft wood, screw-fastening is best.

Bitts can be obtained that drill the screw hole and countersink with one operation. It is always advisable to drill into a hardwood frame for bronze nails; otherwise they will bend when driving. It is claimed they hold better if the correct size hole is used than without drilling.

Riveted plank fastenings are practically a thing of the past except in rowboats. There is really little advantage in this type of fastening, and it involves a great deal of labor.

With the small plywood boat the so-called ring nails, generally bronze, are advisable rather than screws. They effect a saving in time and cost but should be more closely spaced, about 2½″, for instance, for ¼″ plywood and 3″ for ⅜″.

8/ FINISHING THE HULL

NOW THAT THE HULL is planked and fastenings plugged or holes filled flush, it must be smoothed off, caulked or wedged, the seams filled and painted. It is customary to plane the seams roughly before caulking so that the seams when caulked will be of somewhat uniform depth for the final dressing off.

CAULKING

Caulking is not a big job, and if the amateur can have this done by a professional the expense will be relatively small and he will be assured of a good job. However, he may elect to do this himself, and a few words on how it should be done may be helpful.

Prepared caulking cotton is used. It comes in loose strands, and in some brands these strands are just the right size for the average seam; in others they must be separated into smaller ones. Try to obtain the former. A regular caulking iron, small size, is of course used, and if much caulking is to be done a small or boat builder's caulking mallet should be obtained.

The cotton is not driven in straight ribbands but tucked in the seam in small loops or tucks, the size and number of which are governed by the size of the seam. The important knack attained by practice is to govern the amount of cotton to suit the seam; too much will choke it, in which case it is almost impossible to make a finished job. Hard pounding is not required and it only bruises the plank. When there is no seam or where the seam is too small (there are always some like this) it will be necessary to "dum" a seam first, which really means make a seam by driving in the iron and knocking it loose again.

The caulker tucks in a row of tucks for a foot or two with light taps and then goes back and drives the cotton home. Some seams will be found open all the way through and these must be choked—that is, the quantity of cotton must be sufficient to fill the seam without driving through. One thread of cotton is considered sufficient for planking up to about 1¼" or a little more and two threads in heavier planking.

79

PAYING AND FILLING THE SEAMS

After caulking, the seams must be payed—that is, painted—and if a patent seam composition is used, whatever coating is recommended. Care must be taken that the cotton is well painted; some careful builders pay the seams twice. Painting the cotton locks it in the seam and to some extent prevents moisture from penetrating the cotton and rotting it. Seams below the waterline where copper paint will be used are usually payed the same as above. All excess oil must be wiped off the planking with a kerosene-soaked rag, as the oil will prevent copper paint from sticking. However, as most jobs are planed off after puttying, this is generally not necessary.

If wedged, the surplus is roughly trimmed off with a chisel and then a plane; this should be done before the glue hardens. Work boats generally use a mixture of Portland cement and sand on the bottom. No pounding should be done on the boat until it sets up.

The hull may be planed and sanded either before or after the seams are filled; the latter method, I believe, produces a smoother job with less labor. There are several excellent seam compositions for filling seams and nail holes, sold under various trade names. The builder may use one of these or use white lead putty. The common glazing putty will not do; it contains an inferior oil which will penetrate through the paint in brown streaks. White lead putty is made by mixing linseed oil putty with an equal part (in weight) of white lead, either powdered or paste. Some whiting will be needed to make the composition workable, without which it is too sticky to handle. Some add a little varnish and dryer, the latter to make it set up quickly. The putty or composition must be pressed well into the seam with a putty knife or a putty gun. This tool is much like a push-type grease gun and is made from a piece of one-inch brass pipe with a wooden plunger. One end of the pipe is flattened to about ¼", and this is slid along the seam while pressure is applied by the plunger. If the job is large it will pay to make one of these tools; the putty knife, however, probably packs the seam more throughly.

FINISHING THE HULL

A wood smoothing plane, if available, is the best tool for this purpose. Set it fine and plane diagonally across the grain first; this is called traversing. Finish up by planing fore and aft. The plane bitt must not be rounding, and some even use a hollow plane on the bilge.

A fairly hard wood can be scraped before sanding, but this is not practical with cedar, which is sanded first across the grain to remove plane marks and then finished fore and aft. The hull, however, must be planed smooth and fair to the hand, as about all that can be expected of sanding is the removal of the plane marks. It is well worth spending a little extra effort on this job, since little can be done later to rectify a poorly finished hull. A disc sander is a dangerous tool here and may result in a lot of circular gouges. However, a belt sander can be used to advantage.

PAINTING THE HULL

The old days of mixing your own paint, using white lead and linseed oil, are long gone and probably for the better. Good modern marine paint is far superior. Plenty of time should be allowed between coats. Sand lightly between each coat, and if the paint sands off in the form of dust it is dry enough to paint again; if not, sanding should be postponed until it is. Three coats are about the least that can be applied and secure a good job; generally four or more are necessary for a really nice finish. A flat paint is used between priming and finishing coats, a paint that sands smoothly and fills in the small imperfections. After the priming coat the hull should be glazed—that is, the dents in seams, nail holes and other imperfections smoothed over with a paste. This can be made from the white lead putty by adding a little dryer and white lead and bringing it to paste form. Obtained commercially, it is termed surfacing putty. It is applied with a broad putty knife and when dry sanded off with the sanding of the prime coat. Do not allow it to become too dry and hard, however. There are several excellent prepared smoothing or glazing compounds on the market.

The finish coat is much a matter of choice; it may be a high-gloss enamel or a semi-gloss paint. As the enamel is difficult to apply and requires experience to handle, I would advise a good semi-gloss paint. A good hull paint is non-bilging, waterproof and hard enough to resist abrasion and does not stain easily from dirty water running down the sides.

A paint roller can be used to advantage on the topsides. Generally one man applies the paint with the roller, followed closely by another smoothing it out with a brush.

Below the waterline fewer pains are taken; a reasonably smooth surface is all that is required. Copper or other anti-fouling paint is of course used here. Three coats are applied, the last coat five or six hours before launching. Iron rudders, skegs, etc., should be painted with some patent underwater metal paint. There are several brands that resist galvanic action and are much better than the old stand-by, red lead.

THE WATERLINE

Figure 66 shows how the waterline is placed on the boat. Straight-edges are tacked up and leveled across at each end of the boat. The chalk line is first stretched so that it touches about amidships, and then as one man moves the end in toward the

FIG. 66. Placing water line

boat the other drives small finish nails just under the line. Another method is for one to sight across the top of the straight-edge and chalkline while the other places his pencil on the hull and moves it up and down as directed. A batten is tacked to the spots and the line marked in with a raze knife, or a short "back saw" will do. The painted waterline or top of bottom paint should be several inches above the load waterline, higher forward than aft.

THE STEM BAND

The nicest stem band for power boats is of cast manganese bronze. A simple wood pattern is made, fitting it to the boat. As this is generally very long and slender it can be made in two lengths with a short scarf joint (see Fig. 67). It should be fastened with countersunk bronze screws, and the face of the casting must not be much wider than the head of the screw, though some overlap can be filed off.

Second best would be a bronze half round, though this is generally difficult to obtain and brass is resorted to. Brass, however, deteriorates in salt water, as it contains a fairly large amount of zinc.

Galvanized steel half round may be all right in fresh water, but the galvanizing soon disappears in salt water and rust sets in.

VARNISHING

Either interior or exterior varnish, or bright work, as it is called, is handled about as follows. After staining, wood filler is applied, a liquid filler for soft woods

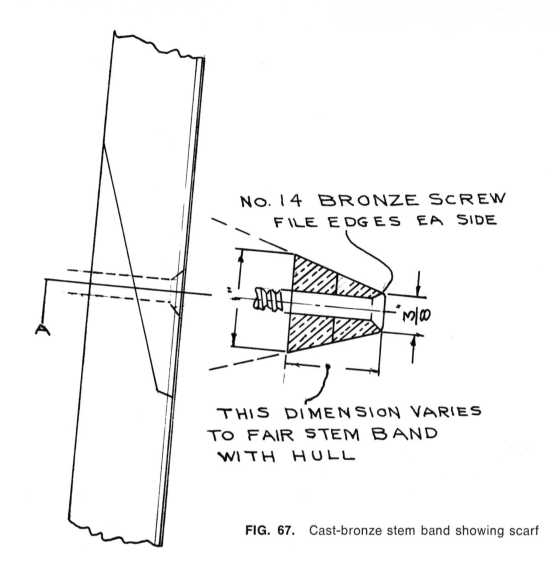

NO. 14 BRONZE SCREW
FILE EDGES EA SIDE

THIS DIMENSION VARIES
TO FAIR STEM BAND
WITH HULL

FIG. 67. Cast-bronze stem band showing scarf

and paste filler for hard woods. When this is almost dry, wipe with clean burlap, a coarse cloth, or excelsior, and after it has dried thoroughly it should be rubbed down with fine sandpaper.

The first coat of varnish should be thinned with about one-fifth turpentine; allow this to dry thoroughly and sand with fine sandpaper. Two or more subsequent coats are necessary to properly protect the surface, sanding between coats, and the final coat should be flowed on and not brushed out too thin. Use only the best spar varnish, which will be found only too short-lived at best. Synthetic varnishes seem to outlast by far those made from tung oil.

Hardwood may be stained to any color desired. A combination filler-stain combines the two operations. Filler is never applied to spars and seldom to decks, the varnish being applied directly to the bare surface.

PREPARED PAINT

As much of the boat paint used today comes prepared in the can ready for use, it is best to follow the manufacturer's recommendation in applying it. The methods mentioned above are what might be termed standard practice. A word of caution as to copper paint: Do not thin it with turpentine or oil. Some use kerosene, but the manufacturer's recommendations in this respect should be followed.

PAINTS

There are two types of anti-fouling bottom paints. One effects its purpose by sluffing off as the growths attempt to adhere and the other by its poisonous content. The latter has a hard surface and is used where skin friction is a factor and where boats are in and out of the water frequently; it is also the most costly.

On metal hulls one or more barrier coats should be applied first. The various manufacturers have done extensive experimentation to arrive at the best possible procedure and are quite free with booklets on the application of their products.

Color is often impregnated in the resin where fiberglass is used, though I have noted that several shops seem to consider painting the surface instead as most satisfactory. The impregnated surface becomes dull and eventually requires painting.

Topside paints and those used for the exterior of the superstructure should under many conditions contain a chemical to prevent a fungus growth that turns white to gray or brown in tidal water where low tides expose a muddy beach. Where the boat may be operated in the vicinity of pulp or paper mills, special paints can be had that will prevent discoloring.

9/ DECK FRAME AND DECK

THE MOST DIFFICULT PART OF BOAT BUILDING CONCERNS, of course, the hull. When this is completed, deck beams, house trunks, etc., and finish are more or less just good joinery. There are good and poor practices in all these things, and it is the purpose here to show the better way or what is considered more or less standard practice.

SHELF AND CLAMP

As shown in the illustrations, there are several methods of handling these. However, with the plywood deck or sub-deck a very strong job results if the beams are hung under the shelf and the plywood glued and fastened to shelf and beams. This also provides something to fasten the top of the sheer strake and frame heads to. Forward, where there is a great deal of curve, the frames are notched or let into the shelf, and this is often done full length of the hull. Where the sides are fairly straight, short pieces can be fitted between the frames instead; frame ends are well suited for this.

BEAMS

Figure 29 shows how the crown or camber of the deck beams is laid out; a pattern is made to this crown, or the widest beam may be used as a pattern. Where excessive crown is not required for headroom a good rule for small boats is ½" crown per foot of total width; thus an eight-foot beam would be crowned 4". This diminishes for larger boats, and a sixteen-foot beam would have about ¼" per foot or even less, perhaps ³⁄₁₆". Some builders save lumber by sawing the beam material in two to the required crown and glueing it together again as in Fig. 68. If properly glued it will not weaken the beams. Beams should be sawed from edge grain stock where possible, as it is stronger and less likely to split.

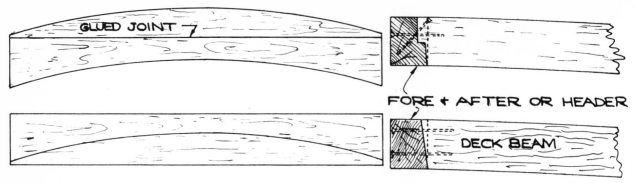

FIG. 68. Sawing out material for beams and glueing up   **FIG. 69.** Headers and half-beam end fit

Laminated beams, while not widely used, are sometimes specified. These are made up of three of more glued-up layers bent over a form and are stronger than the sawed type. They should be bent to slightly more crown than required on the boat, as they will straighten a bit when taken off the form. The additional labor required in this type of beam is against its more general use.

Since one function of deck beams is to tie the boat together they should be well fastened at the ends to shelf or clamp. One sometimes sees beams landed on a narrow clamp and merely edge-nailed into it and with the fastening at the very end where it has little holding power.

Figure 69 shows how headers at deck openings and half beams are fitted. The upper illustration is used where much weight is likely to be put on the deck; the lower one is all right for light work. Where deck openings are long, and with single caulked deck, tie rods should be placed from header to outside of frame and are generally shown on the plans every third beam or so apart. This applies only to caulked decks; obviously a plywood deck cannot spread.

Where possible it is good practice to place a temporary stringer down the center under the beams until the deck is laid, and bulkheads should be fitted before the deck goes on.

Knees are seldom used today, but they are of two types, hanging and lodging. Hanging knees are hung under the beams and extend down the frame of the boat. Lodging knees are used in sailboats and are placed horizontally at ends of beams and as ties between beams and hull and headers, etc. Where there is much curve to the frame a pattern is made from which the knee is sawed. It is then planed fair where it fits against the beam and the sides scribed in while clamped in place. Screw bolts are the best knee fastenings, though riveted bolts are sometimes used.

Plywood gussets have largely replaced knees, and plywood decks have in general done away with lodging knees. Sometimes several layers of plywood are glued together to form a knee and the exposed edge covered with an ⅛″ strip

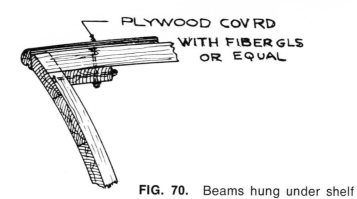

FIG. 70. Beams hung under shelf

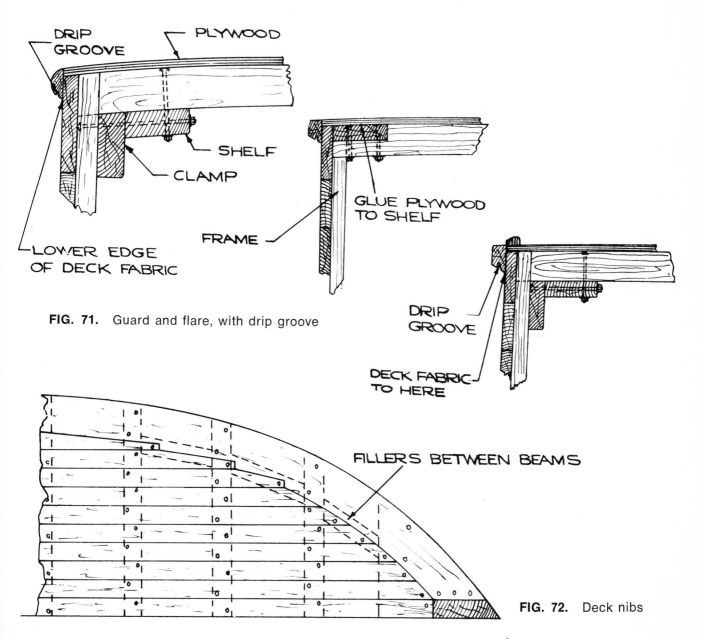

FIG. 71. Guard and flare, with drip groove

FIG. 72. Deck nibs

of hardwood. More often a single thickness is used and glued and screw-fastened alongside beam and frame or in the superstructure beam and house stiffener. This makes a very light and strong knee with very little fitting.

LAYING THE DECK

There are two types of deck, the fabric-covered and the caulked. The former is less expensive, lighter in weight, and seldom troubles the owner with leaks. The caulked deck has of course the nicest appearance, but I think all sailboat owners will agree that the single-thickness deck is hard to keep tight. To be practical such a deck should be at least 1¼″ thick.

The so-called caulked deck with a plywood sub-deck under it eliminates the leak problem and also results in a more rigid structure. The sub-deck must be well fastened to the beams, shelf, etc., and should be glued to them; this is of particular importance at the plywood butts. The plywood sheets must be laid with the long sides fore and aft.

The teak deck is laid in Thiokol or similar compound, being sure there are no voids. This is a very messy job but becomes less so with a little experience. The seams are not caulked but are filled with the same compound, and the teak should be screw-fastened to the beams, etc., and plugged (see Fig. 72).

There is a manufactured teak decking about a half-inch thick and about four inches wide with a fake seam in the center simulating two-inch-wide decking. The double butt ends are an eyesore. If one half is cut back about eight inches a much more shipshape appearance results.

Guards should be laid in heavy paint or, better still, a bedding compound, and where there is much flare, as in Fig. 71, it is best to flatten off or plumb up a face for the guard; otherwise it is almost impossible to pull it tight on the lower edge. Screw fastenings are always used.

SYNTHETIC FABRICS

These have largely replaced canvas for deck coverings, and since they do not rot they are generally considered superior.

There are many of these, though fiberglass seems most universally in use. Instead of considering some of them as deck coverings only, they are often used to cover the entire hull in plywood construction. In fact, fiberglass can be the entire structural material, as is elaborated in Chapter 16.

Fiberglass seems to adhere better to some woods than others, and sometimes trouble is experienced with Western red cedar. Care must be taken in using any of these materials. Even the professional sometimes has trouble, and it is often hard for him to explain bubbles appearing in the finished product, though they are not difficult to take out.

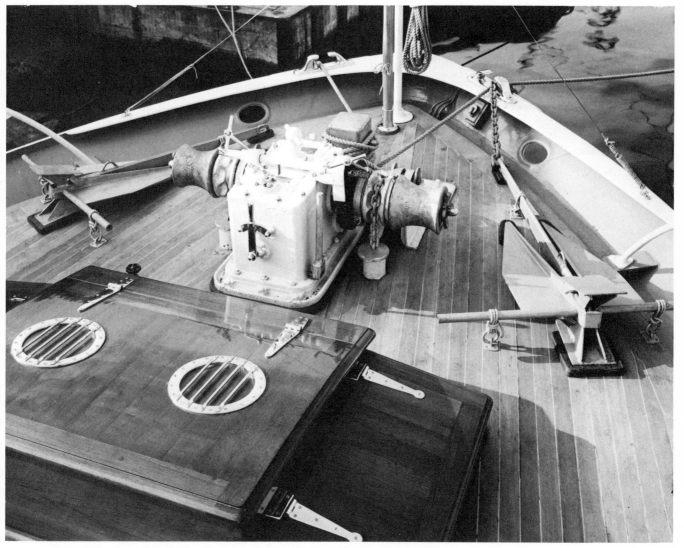

FIG. 73. Nicely laid teak deck showing nib ends of deck plank

Fiberglass cloth only is used, and eight-ounce is considered about the right weight for hull and deck use. I suppose the best advice would be to follow the manufacturer's instructions as closely as possible. In some places there are professional fiberglassers, and often these are employed by the boat shop on the premise that they can do it better and at less cost. Some builders first apply a thin layer of fiberglass mat which no doubt produces a superior job.

THE CAULKED DECK

Caulked decks may be sprung to the shape of the covering board or cabin sides or laid straight fore and aft and nibbed as shown in Fig. 72. With the sprung deck a wide or king plank is placed in the center and decking nibbed into it and covering board. Fillers must be fitted between the beams to support and provide a fastening for the nibs. Three or four strakes are laid and fitted at a time, wedged up tight and fastened. As beams are generally soft wood, screws form the best fastening, though nails are sometimes used and holes are always plugged with deck plugs set in shellac or glue. Deck plugs may be purchased at the ship chandlery, or the builder may make them with a plug cutter. It is always advisable to try the plug first to see that it is a tight fit, as plug bitts and plug cutters vary in size.

A proper seam composition for decking is a knotty problem. Putty will not do, since it requires a more or less elastic composition that will adhere tightly to the walls of the seam and stretch and compress with the going and coming of the wood. There are various patented compositions used with good result, and the builder will have to select one of these.

The deck is finished with plane, scraped and sanded, and then either varnished or oiled, though a teak deck is often left bare and holystoned. The varnish finish is of course far the nicest but requires a great deal of care, will not stand up under severe conditions, and is slippery when wet. There is a linseed-oil derivative named Liquid Rawhide which, though not as bright as varnish, is less slippery and seems almost impervious to salt water. Many of our sailors use a mixture of Stockholm tar and boiled linseed oil, half and half, on pine or Douglas fir decks. This gives the deck a brownish color. Others have pet formulas based on the above but with the addition of other ingredients, including litharge.

What was said about caulking the hull will apply also to the deck.

CABIN TRUNKS

Three methods in fitting cabin trunks are shown in Fig. 74. A rabbeted coaming is used with the caulked deck, and the sill or fore and after below the coaming should be wide enough to form a backing for the caulking as shown. With the fabric-covered deck the trunk may be placed on top of the fiberglass or other covering, or the trunk may be screw-fastened against the shelf. The former is used with a heavier trunk where it is possible to edge bolt, and it is set in a bedding compound. Where the trunk, usually plywood, is placed alongside the shelf, the deck fabric should be carried up trunk sides, as shown, and trunks should have closely spaced fastenings and be set in bedding compound. Sometimes a quarter-round is substituted, and though tight at first, it will eventually shrink away from the wood and leak.

Often a cabin trunk must be made in two or more widths, in which case the joint should be grooved and a spline placed in the groove. This is not so necessary with soft woods, which are usually painted and hold glue well, but some hardwoods, particularly teak, do not hold glue well and may open up at the joint.

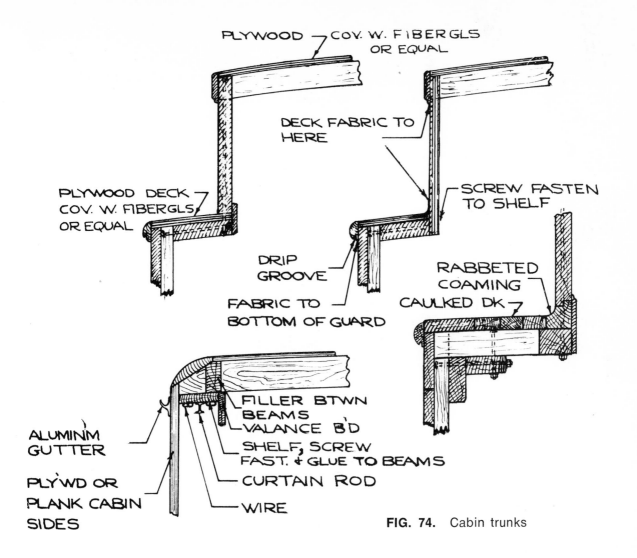

PLYWOOD — COV. W. FIBERGLS OR EQUAL

DECK FABRIC TO HERE

SCREW FASTEN TO SHELF

PLYWOOD DECK COV. W. FIBERGLS. OR EQUAL

DRIP GROOVE

RABBETED COAMING

CAULKED DK.

FABRIC TO BOTTOM OF GUARD

FILLER BTWN BEAMS

VALANCE B'D

SHELF, SCREW FAST. & GLUE TO BEAMS

ALUMINM GUTTER

CURTAIN ROD

PLY'WD OR PLANK CABIN SIDES

WIRE

FIG. 74. Cabin trunks

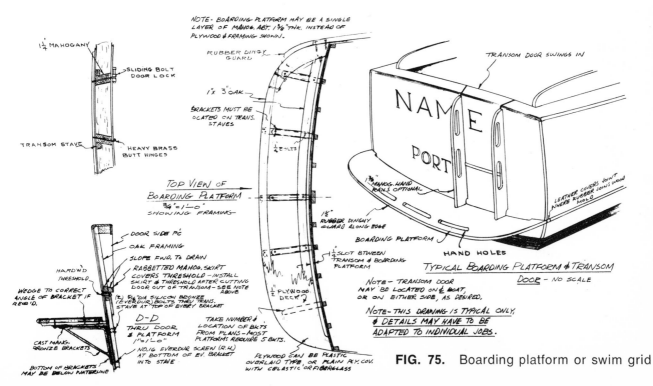

NOTE- BOARDING PLATFORM MAY BE A SINGLE LAYER OF MAHOG. ABT. 1 ⅜" THK. INSTEAD OF PLYWOOD & FRAMING SHOWN.

1¼ MAHOGANY

SLIDING BOLT DOOR LOCK

RUBBER DINGY GUARD

1" x 3" OAK

BRACKETS MUST BE LOCATED ON TRANS. STAVES

TRANSOM STAVE

HEAVY BRASS BUTT HINGES

½" BOLTS

TOP VIEW OF BOARDING PLATFORM ¾"=1'-0" SHOWING FRAMING

DOOR SIDE PC

OAK FRAMING

SLOPE FWD. TO DRAIN

RABBETTED MAHOG. SKIRT COVERS THRESHOLD - INSTALL SKIRT & THRESHOLD AFTER CUTTING DOOR OUT OF TRANSOM — SEE NOTE ABOVE

HARDWD. THRESHOLD

WEDGE TO CORRECT ANGLE OF BRACKET IF REQ'D.

(2) ⅜" DIA. SILICON BRONZE (EVERDUR) BOLTS THRU TRANS. STAVE AT TOP OF EVERY BRACKET

D-D THRU DOOR & PLATFORM 1"=1'-0"

CAST MANG. BRONZE BRACKETS

NO.16 EVERDUR SCREW (R.H.) AT BOTTOM OF EV. BRACKET INTO STAVE

BOTTOM OF BRACKETS MAY BE BELOW WATERLINE

TAKE NUMBER & LOCATION OF BLTS FROM PLANS—MOST PLATFORMS REQUIRE 5 BLTS.

PLYWOOD CAN BE PLASTIC OVERLAID TYPE, OR PLAIN PLY. COV. WITH CELASTIC OR FIBERGLASS

½" PLYWOOD DECK

1¼ SLOT BTWEEN TRANSOM & BOARDING PLATFORM

1⅛" RUBBER DINGY GUARD ALONG EDGE

TRANSOM DOOR SWINGS IN

NAME

PORT

1¼" MAHOG. HAND RAILS OPTIONAL

LEATHER COVERS JOINT WHERE RUBBER JOINS WOOD MOLD

BOARDING PLATFORM

HAND HOLES

TYPICAL BOARDING PLATFORM & TRANSOM DOOR - NO SCALE

NOTE- TRANSOM DOOR MAY BE LOCATED ON ℄ BOAT, OR ON EITHER SIDE, AS DESIRED.

NOTE- THIS DRAWING IS TYPICAL ONLY, & DETAILS MAY HAVE TO BE ADAPTED TO INDIVIDUAL JOBS.

FIG. 75. Boarding platform or swim grid

FIG. 76. (Above) Aft stateroom showing curtain valance board, beam soles under beams, and companion steps

FIG. 77. (Opposite, above) Control stand showing small switches for navigation lights, windshield wipers, etc. The side switches are for bilge pumps and the valve handle above for windshield squirts. *Photo by Ray Krantz*

FIG. 78. (Opposite, below) Flying bridge showing seat with life preserver locker underneath, also hinged mast and clear-view windshield without wood frame at top. *Photo by Ray Krantz*

THE BOARDING PLATFORM AND TRANSOM DOOR

The first boarding platform, to my knowledge, was an innovation born of necessity. A West Coast boater was faced with getting his crippled wife aboard his new boat from a dinghy; hence the door. The door opening should be framed in the transom frame insofar as practical and the opening cut out after it is planked. Otherwise, there may be an unfair spot at each side of the opening.

The slot between boarding platform and transom is to relieve the pressure from a following sea. Even this, however, has proven inadequate under the most adverse conditions, and one or two have been torn off by the sea. A slatted platform, though more costly to construct and difficult to keep looking sharp, should eliminate this hazard. The slats, usually of teak, run thwartships and are about 1″ x 1¼″ on edge with about ⅞″ between. Hand holes should always be installed as they may someday prevent a tragedy.

10/PLYWOOD CONSTRUCTION

PLYWOOD IS AN EXCELLENT BOAT-BUILDING MATERIAL. It has some limitations in shape; therefore almost all are V-bottom. It can of course be employed in the most difficult of shapes by lamination, and boats as long as seventy feet have been so constructed.

It appeals to the amateur builder, eliminating as it does plank shaping, planking seams and caulking them, and the rather tedious job of smoothing and sanding the hull. Well fastened and with generous application of glue, it makes a strong and lightweight hull.

While plywood is generally associated with small boats, using orthodox methods, cruisers up to forty or even fifty feet are quite practical. An illustration is shown of a fifty-foot Diesel cruiser built in Portugal, and the plans shown are of a twenty-six-footer.

Some plywood, ⅜″ in particular, is manufactured using three plies only, the center ply very thick with a thin ply on each side. This would apply to ⅜″ or thicker and should be avoided.

Hulls are almost always longitudinally framed—that is, chine and stringers form longitudinal framing—and widely spaced frames and the bulkheads give transverse strength. Often the plywood planking or skin is fastened to the longitudinal members only, except of course at stem and transom.

The boat is lofted as with any other V-bottom. However, the forward part of the bottom must be conically developed, or the plywood in this section put on in narrower widths with the seams landing on the longitudinals. Shown is a typical conical development; this should be shown in the design, however.

CONICAL DEVELOPMENT

Conical development is a trial-and-error process. First, fairly close buttocks are drawn in the plan view and the body plan. In Fig. 81 conical lines 2 and 4 were drawn intersecting the stations at rabbet and at chine and meeting at point A.

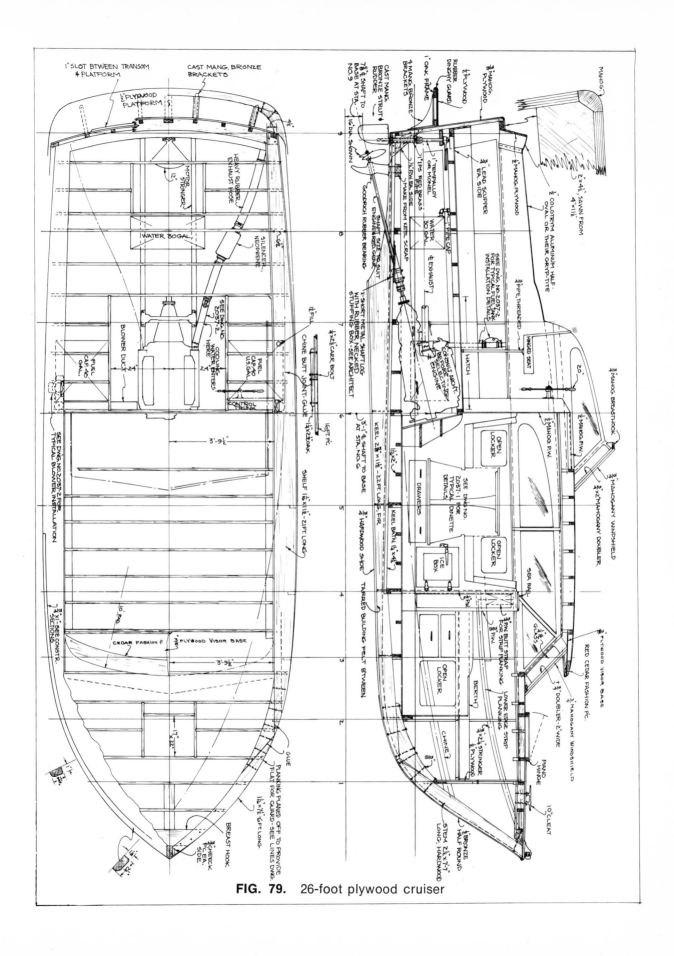

FIG. 79. 26-foot plywood cruiser

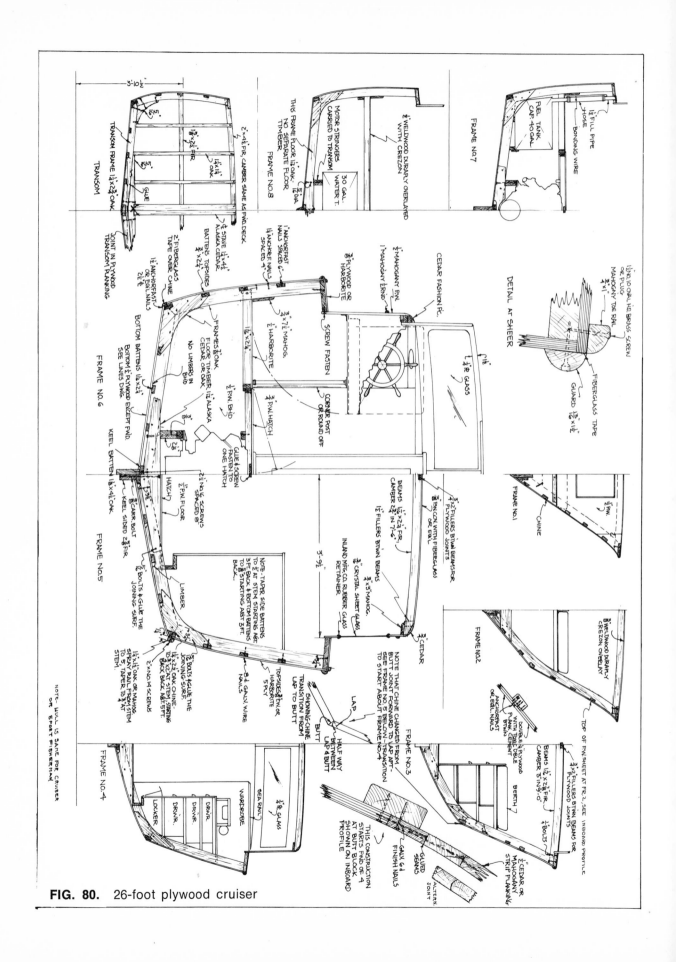

FIG. 80. 26-foot plywood cruiser

Intersecting the rabbet at the stations was just a good way to start and disregarded later in the development. Lines 1 and 3 are next. A vertical line is projected down from the intersection. Lines 1A, 2A, 3, and 4A are next and are drawn through the intersections of 1, 2, 3, and 4 with the rabbet. Chances are they will not meet at the downward projection of A. You must size up the situation and move point A up or down, out or in, where it would seem to work out better. Should a slight change in the rabbet line rectify the situation, this is quite in order, and it has been my experience that if some of the intersections are slightly off this can be disregarded.

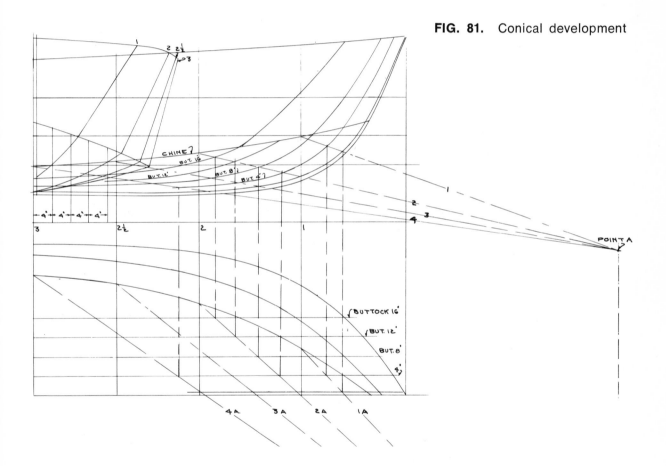

FIG. 81. Conical development

The side planking seems to pull in easily at a convex transom and no development here is generally required.

The developed surface results unavoidably in a rather full bow and, by virtue of its shape, a strong one.

Provided the boat is not too large, there is a real advantage in setting it up upside down. The limiting factor is turning it over, and if this is done after the bottom only has been planked it will be much lighter.

Until the planking stage, construction is identical to V-bottom construction, Chapter 5 in this book.

It is sometimes possible to obtain plywood in long lengths. These really consist of the standard eight-foot panels joined together by scarfing; twelve feet is the longest the writer is aware of in one piece. Some builders have resorted to doing their own scarfing. This requires careful shaping, a positive clamping arrangement, and the proper temperature. All of this, however, is usually attainable without great outlay.

The standard eight-foot length will result in an equally strong hull by the use of butt straps fitted between the stringers. (See illustration of a typical butt strap.) Should the entire hull be fiberglassed, the butt joints need no special

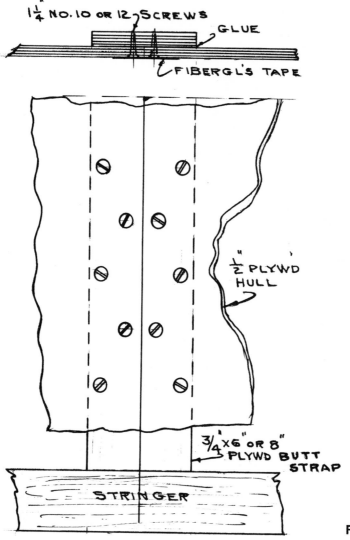

FIG. 82. Planking butt strap

treatment, but if not, then they should be covered with fiberglass tape two or more inches wide and feathered at the edges with sandpaper so as to be as inconspicuous as possible after the hull is painted. They may show slightly under certain light conditions but will insure watertightness and hide the joint.

Planking should start with the forward end, securing the piece first at the stem and bending it in place. Use a long piece for topsides to pass the hard bend, if obtainable. A pattern of heavy building paper should be made, at least for the forward bottom plank, to transfer the correct shape to the plywood. Bedding compound should be used liberally at stem, keel batten, chine, etc., for watertightness, and waterproof glue on the longitudinals and shelf. The plywood should be fastened before the glue hardens, and fastenings are invariably screws or the nonferrous ring nail. The latter is really more practical except perhaps when fastening into very soft wood such as spruce. The plywood is generally quite thin and therefore requires that the fastenings be closely spaced, about 2″ to 2½″ for ¼″ and 3″ for ½″. This does not apply, however, to the longitudinals or shelf, where the spacing can be twice the above.

As with the butts, the chine should be fiberglassed to assure watertightness, as should the ends at the transom, provided it is not finished bright—that is, varnished. Whether or not to depend on the compound for watertightness at the keel is a moot question, and a light thread of caulking cotton here would assure it. Water seems to have the ability to creep in where one would almost swear it could not. Where the keel is superimposed over the planking, no caulking should be required.

There are special sealers recommended for plywood to "tame" the grain. Whether or not one is used, the hull should be given several coats of flat white to hide the grain, sanding between coats.

Most hulls are of fir plywood, and this material unfortunately has a grain-raising tendency. This may appear after the boat has been in the water a short time. At the end of the first season the hull can be sanded and given a coat or two of flat white and refinished, and this should end the grain rise.

Mahogany plywood—in particular Utile African mahogany—does not have this fault, though it is a bit heavier, if weight is a major consideration. However, being stronger, it can be a little thinner.

More often than not, the plywood planking runs by at the stem and there is no rabbet. The ends are dressed off to a flat surface which is capped with oak or other hardwood set in a bedding compound and screw-fastened. As it extends down over the curved forefoot, it must either be steam bent (if oak) or it can be laminated, using thin strips and waterproof glue.

Often it is easier to band-saw this part from a wider piece and fit it to the forefoot. The stem band should be half round and not half oval or it can be cast. Bronze is almost essential in salt water, fastened with bronze screws.

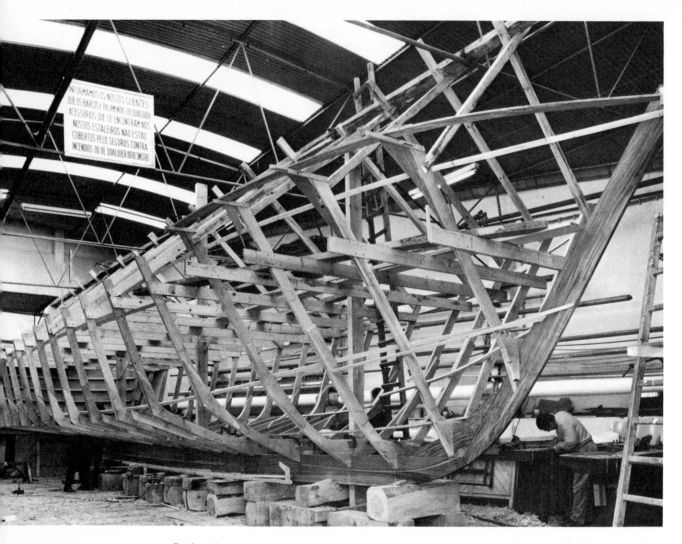

It is always advisable to cover the exposed plywood ends or edges, as for instance at deck and planking where water may seep into the end grain and cause the paint to blister and, worse still, encourage dry rot. Generally the decks are fiberglass or equal, and this can be carried down over the edge to the underside of the guard, protecting both deck and planking.

Something should be said about nail and screw heads in plywood planking. The latter are countersunk just sufficiently to cover them with a thin layer of surfacing compound.

Some do the same with nail heads, using a regular screw head countersink; others use a leather punch or a drill just slightly larger than the nail head. A smooth job cannot be made by simply trying to set the head into the surface of the plywood.

Completing the plywood boat, decks, superstructure, and joiner work is no or very little different than with other types of hull construction.

FIG. 83. (Opposite) 50-foot plywood cruiser in frame

FIG. 84. (Above) Same 50-foot plywood cruiser planked. Lisbon, Portugal.

11/ FINISHING THE INTERIOR

IN THE DAYS OF DONALD MCKAY the shutter or last plank always called for a celebration, usually somewhat bacchanalian. When the boat builder has the hull finished, the deck on, and is ready to move inside, he feels justified in doing a little celebrating. It seems then that the end is in sight and the realization of his dreams almost an actuality.

The fitting of berths, lockers, dish racks, stove, sink, etc., should not require much elaboration, but there are a few items that should be touched upon. One of these is ceiling. A common mistake in the past has been to overdo this matter, ceiling the boat up tight from floor to clamp and even fitting pieces between beams, which effectively shut out all chances of ventilation.

FIG. 85. (Opposite, upper left) Interior showing totem pole boat deck support, curtain valance boards, and pull-out settee which forms double berth. *Photo by Ray Krantz*

FIG. 86. (Opposite, upper right) Transom door, fireplace, locker doors under side deck, hi-low table, and acoustic tile ceiling. *Photo by Ray Krantz*

FIG. 87. (Opposite, middle left) Galley and dinette with one type of dish rack on 38-foot cruiser *Photo by Harry Merrick*

FIG. 88. (Opposite, middle right) Galley has enclosed dish locker over stove, and drawer under stove stores pots and pans. Built-in refrigerator has ice box hardware. *Photo by Jan Fardell*

FIG. 89. (Opposite, lower left) Salon showing curtain valance boards and ceiling treatment *Photo by Harbour and Shipping*

FIG. 90. (Opposite, lower right) Forward view of interior showing stove installation, master switches under steps, and toilet *Photo by Ray Krantz*

CEILING AND VENTILATION

Generally speaking, except where required for strength, a boat should not be ceiled except where the frames are exposed above berths and lockers in the living quarters, and several very nice boats have been built dispensing with even this small amount. All dead-air spaces, such as clothes lockers, beneath berths, etc., should be provided with ventilation: louvers, decorative cutouts, screened doors, or a screened hole. Some builders use hole or peg board for ceiling, which of course affords excellent ventilation and if tastefully painted is not generally objectionable.

There are now made a wide variety of ornamental screens used in building construction principally for radiator shields. This material forms a very nice-appearing panel for doors and, cut in smaller pieces, can just be tacked over ventilating holes, without trim or molding if desired, using brass escutcheon pins.

As the chain locker is usually poorly ventilated, a small cowl vent that may be replaced with a deck plug will provide excellent ventilation here or in any other similar place, such as the lazarette in a sailboat.

BULKHEADS AND PLYWOOD

The best material for bulkheads where a nice finish is required on both sides is no doubt plywood. Today's waterproof plywood is a reliable material. Alternate soaking and drying and steaming and heating seems to have no effect. The author has tested a sample by nailing it to a pile where it was alternately wet and dry with each tide. Six months of this treatment left the sample practically undamaged. Apparently this material can be used with the utmost confidence under the most adverse conditions. It is sold under several trade names and is, of course, more expensive than the non-waterproof variety. There are many qualities that make its use very desirable. If properly fastened, it is a strength bulkhead. It is superior to tongue and groove in this respect and presents a smooth, easily finished surface; also it is quickly installed. Mahogany or other hardwood faced-plywood, whether painted or finished bright, forms the nicest surface, as it does not have the grain rise that occurs in the rotary-cut fir plywood.

PORT LIGHTS

Round port lights are of two types: inside and outside patterns. The inside pattern or barrel type is generally used in trunk cabins and is of brass or bronze, and the barrel should be of such length that it will project about $\frac{3}{16}''$ outside. A porthole cutter which is much like a large expansion bitt will make the smoothest job if it is available; if not, use a keyhole saw. The outside pattern is used generally through the hull itself and is usually galvanized. These lights can be fitted with a keyhole saw, since no great exactitude is required. Port lights may be installed to hinge up or open sideways as the builder sees fit.

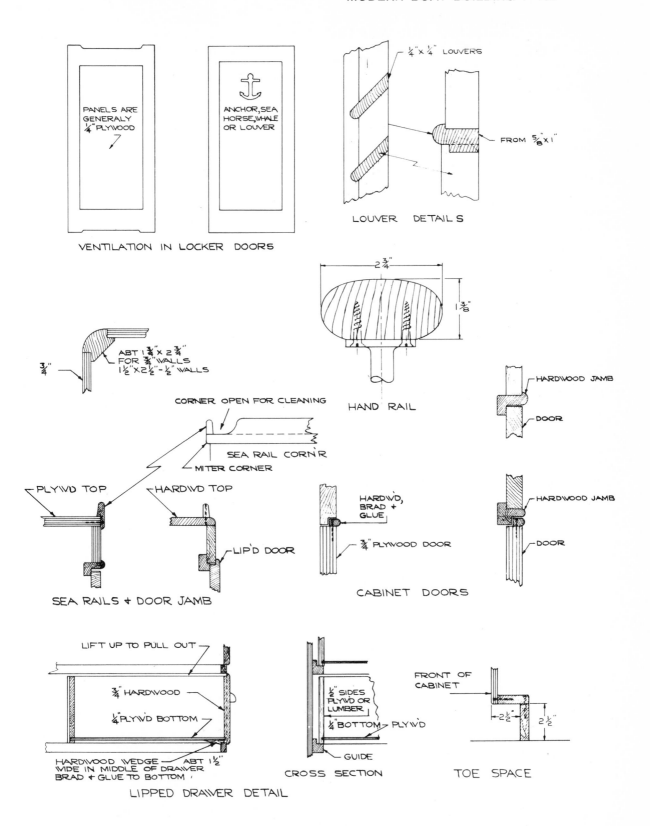

FIG. 91. Joiner details

FIG. 92. Window details and sailboat exhaust

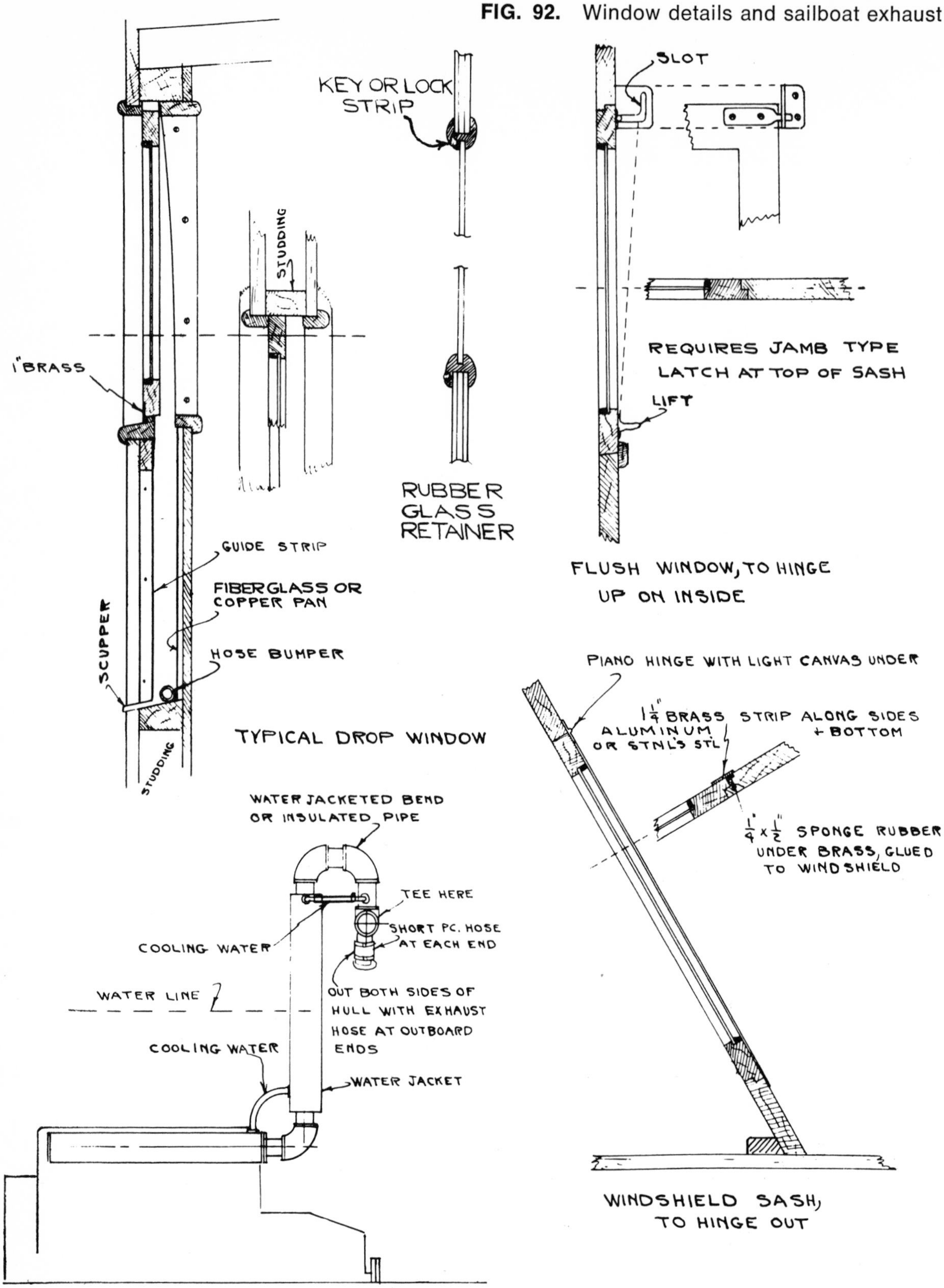

KEY OR LOCK STRIP

SLOT

i" BRASS

STUDDING

RUBBER GLASS RETAINER

REQUIRES JAMB TYPE LATCH AT TOP OF SASH

LIFT

SCUPPER

GUIDE STRIP

FIBERGLASS OR COPPER PAN

HOSE BUMPER

STUDDING

TYPICAL DROP WINDOW

FLUSH WINDOW, TO HINGE UP ON INSIDE

PIANO HINGE WITH LIGHT CANVAS UNDER

1¼" BRASS STRIP ALONG SIDES + BOTTOM

ALUMINUM OR STNL'S STL

¼" x ½" SPONGE RUBBER UNDER BRASS, GLUED TO WINDSHIELD

WATER JACKETED BEND OR INSULATED PIPE

TEE HERE

SHORT PC. HOSE AT EACH END

COOLING WATER

WATER LINE

OUT BOTH SIDES OF HULL WITH EXHAUST HOSE AT OUTBOARD ENDS

COOLING WATER

WATER JACKET

WINDSHIELD SASH, TO HINGE OUT

Rectangular port lights have largely replaced the round, at least in power boats, as the former should be set in bedding compound.

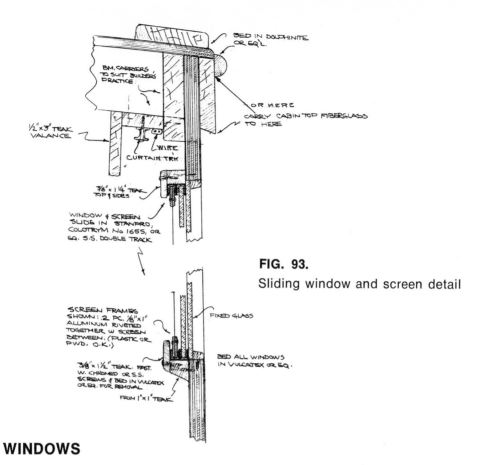

FIG. 93.

Sliding window and screen detail

WINDOWS

Windows to open are always a problem. In Fig. 92 is shown the drop window, which is used generally in double construction where there is ceiling inside and sheathing out with studding between. Copper or fiberglass pockets scuppered outside are almost necessary, though the pocket is sometimes just well painted with asphalt paint. Another type shown is used in single construction. The window must first pull out on top, rise clear below, and then hinge up and secure to the beams above with a hook. There are various types of pivots and hangers, but most are quite similar to the one shown. There must be a knob or handle on top of the sash also in order to pull this part out.

There is now available an excellent factory-made window with aluminum frames similar to those seen on coaches and buses. It then becomes necessary only to cut the hole and fasten in the aluminum frame. They will not, of course, accommodate to any but the slightest bend or curve.

Adapted also from the automobile industry is the rubber glass retainer as shown in Fig. 92. This is available for cabin sides from ½″ to at least ¾″ and for ³⁄₁₆″ or ¼″ glass. It is also available for the thin metal house. This is no doubt the most economical window of all. It can be obtained with double groove for sliding glass or, if not available, the sliding can be accomplished as in Fig. 93. Be sure to provide an ample drain hole, and the gap between glass must face aft.

There is an argument as to whether to use plate or safety glass. Plate thickness is generally ¼″ and safety ³⁄₁₆″. The former is much stronger and the latter has the shatterproof advantage. There is also tempered glass of astonishing strength.

The windshield sash shown must have a rubber gasket of some sort around sides and bottom with wedge action handles at lower corners to be really watertight; also it is fitted with a quadrant or sliding-rod device to hold it open. There are many other types of windows; many of them, however, are not very practical, and others, such as the sliding sash, hardly need explaining.

SKYLIGHTS

It has been said that all skylights leak. This is more or less true, as driving spray or rain and a stiff wind will blow the water up and under almost any hinged cover unless it can be clamped down on gaskets. However, the one shown is watertight under ordinary conditions and is a standard pattern not too hard to make. The brass strips on the upper edges will lead the drip into the trough; the sides and ends may be dovetailed instead or halved as shown. Teak and mahogany are the best materials for all skylights, doors, and windows, with teak ranking first, and most of these jobs require machinery not generally possessed by the amateur, such as a shaper, tenon machine, etc. While they can be made by hand tools, it is a laborious process and it is difficult to equal the accuracy of modern woodworking machinery. Sometimes part of the work can be done at a cabinet shop and the balance by the builder. The skylight shown would be one of these.

A SLIDING HATCH

A sliding hatch, where feasible, is about the only answer to a watertight opening for a companionway, and details of one of these are shown. The fillers should be fitted between the beams as shown to stop the wind blowing through at the sides and carrying the spray along with it. The slide had best be built right in place, being sure to provide ample play and keeping in mind the fact that, like a drawer, it will swell a little in damp weather. Built as shown, it will give a good account of itself. There are several other very good methods for making a slide, all more or less similar to this one.

HINGED HATCH

This requires less space and is easier to make. Shown is a detail drawing of a typical hinged hatch.

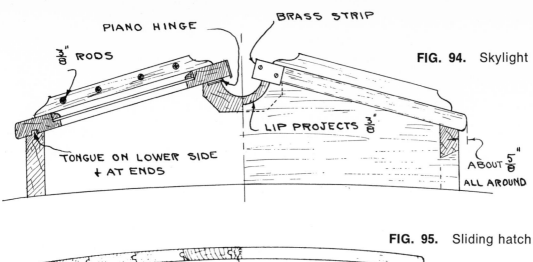

PIANO HINGE   BRASS STRIP

⅜" RODS

FIG. 94. Skylight

LIP PROJECTS ⅜"

TONGUE ON LOWER SIDE
& AT ENDS

ABOUT ⅝"
ALL AROUND

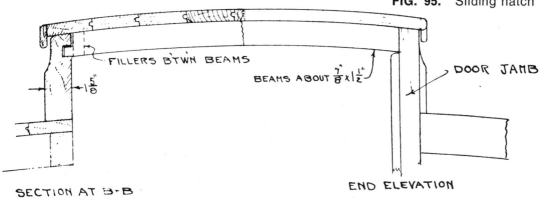

FIG. 95. Sliding hatch

FILLERS B'TW'N BEAMS

BEAMS ABOUT ⅞" x 1½"

DOOR JAMB

1⅝"

SECTION AT B-B

END ELEVATION

FIG. 96. Hinged hatch and companion doorway

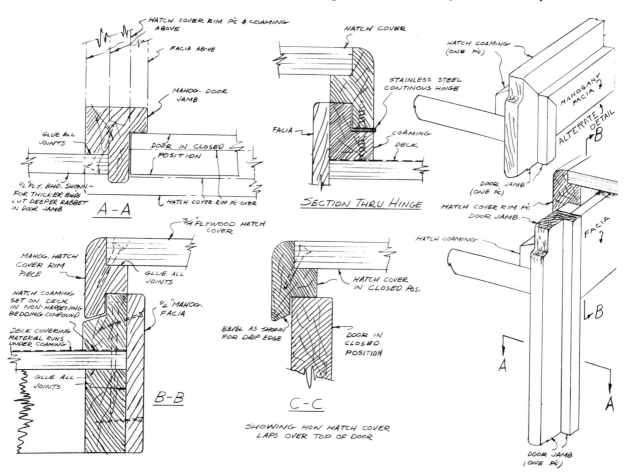

HATCH COVER RIM P'C & COAMING
ABOVE

FACIA ABOVE

MAHOG. DOOR
JAMB

GLUE ALL
JOINTS

DOOR IN CLOSED
POSITION

½ PLY. BH'D. SHOWN -
FOR THICKER BH'D'S
CUT DEEPER RABBET
IN DOOR JAMB

HATCH COVER RIM P'C OVER

A - A

HATCH COVER

STAINLESS STEEL
CONTINUOUS HINGE

FACIA

COAMING
DECK

SECTION THRU HINGE

HATCH COAMING
(ONE P'C)

MAHOGANY
FACIA

ALTERNATE DETAIL

B

DOOR JAMB
(ONE P'C)

HATCH COVER RIM P'C
DOOR JAMB

¾ PLYWOOD HATCH
COVER

MAHOG. HATCH
COVER RIM
PIECE

GLUE ALL
JOINTS

HATCH COAMING
SET ON DECK
IN NON-HARDENING
BEDDING COMPOUND

½" MAHOG.
FACIA

DECK COVERING
MATERIAL RUNS
UNDER COAMING

GLUE ALL
JOINTS

B - B

HATCH COAMING

HATCH COVER
IN CLOSED POS.

BEVEL AS SHOWN
FOR DRIP EDGE

DOOR IN
CLOSED
POSITION

C - C

SHOWING HOW HATCH COVER
LAPS OVER TOP OF DOOR

B

A

A

DOOR JAMB
(ONE P'C)

SPECIAL FITTINGS

Special fittings that cannot be purchased from a ship chandler will crop up on some jobs; struts, for instance, are generally cast for each boat. There are other special fittings of metal, such as rail stanchions, stem bands, and some sailboat fittings, in the same category. A wooden pattern can be made for each of these, and the castings themselves are not expensive. The builder must keep in mind, however, that the pattern must be made so that it can be drawn out of the molding sand by the foundryman. Simple patterns do not offer much of a problem, but the more complicated ones had best be done by a pattern maker.

INSTALLING THE MOTOR

A fine line is stretched through the center of shaft hole and allowed to extend well forward of the motor. From this line the engine beds are installed, allowing at least a half inch for shims between motor and engine bed, more if vibration dampeners are used. Check down from this line to be sure there will be sufficient depth for the motor base. Mark at each end of the shaft log the center of the line and fit stuffing box and stern bearing to these marks. It may be necessary first, however, to square up the ends of the log to take the base. Slip the shaft in place before the final tightening up and place a compound under stuffing box to assure watertightness.

Some builders—and I think the most progressive ones—install shaft and bearings (single screw) while the backbone lies flat on the sawhorses. It is then easier to fair off the aft end, with no time wasted getting in and out of the boat.

Vibration dampeners will help smooth out performance. If they are used their thickness is allowed for, and unless they are fitted with adjusting bolts the wood shims are still required. Some motors are fitted with jacking screws; these are a great help in lining up the motor.

The shaft can be slipped in place, the coupling slipped on, and the motor placed on the bed. Some face the aft coupling mounted on shaft in a lathe. The motor is then wedged up so that the coupling faces come together properly. Feelers, which are very thin leaves of metal graduated in thousandths of an inch, are slipped between the coupling faces to line up the couplings exactly. The shaft should be turned to see that the couplings line up in all positions. Hardwood shims are made to fit between motor and bed, and then galvanized sheet-metal shims are placed between motor and wood shims if needed in bringing the motor into final alignment before bolting down. Bronze hanger bolts are used for bolting down, and these have two nuts on top so that the motor may be removed without disturbing the bolts.

The same process is used with a twin screw job, except that the strut will take the place of the outboard bearing, and if it is babbitted the babbitting is done with shaft in place. The babbitted bearing, however, has been almost

FIG. 97. Outboard motor bracket and cockpit locker

universally replaced by the rubber bearing. Where the motor is located forward, requiring an intermediate shaft and bearing, the line must be used for lining up this shaft also. As it generally passes through a bulkhead just aft of the motor, a centering cross mark is placed here. The tail shaft is set first, the intermediate shaft lined up to it, coupling to coupling, and then the motor lined up to forward coupling as before.

FUEL LINES AND TANKS

Gas lines should always be copper tubing and use the flanged or flared fittings, not the ferrule type; the former cannot pull apart. Shellac or gasket cement, not paint, should be used in making up joints, as they will not dissolve in contact with gasoline. A shut-off value should be placed at all tanks and one at the carburetor. Tanks should always fill from outside, with a tight connection between deck and tank. Vents of copper tubing must be run from the top of the tank to the outside of the boat and should be fitted with screens. In sailboats it is often necessary to run them up inside the trunk and then out with a small gooseneck at the upper end.

Diesel fuel lines, while generally of copper tubing, are sometimes of ungalvanized or black pipe or stainless-steel tubing. Often a short section of flexible tubing manufactured for the purpose is used at the motor end of the fuel line.

Whether Diesel or gasoline, there should be an adequate filter and water trap or separator in the line, and all lines should be secured in place with clips.

The illustration shows a typical gasoline motor installation. The wire static electricity jumpers over the hose are not generally used with Diesel installation. The National Fire Protection Association has published a booklet advocating many safety practices in engine and tank installation, and a copy of this book would inform the builder if he has the safest of installations. See "Ventilating Motor Compartment" for address. It is recommended that the for'd vents face aft and vice versa; however, where they are closely coupled recirculation may occur.

Gasoline tanks are generally of galvanized iron or, more properly, mild steel. The better tank is a welded one, hot-dip galvanized after welding. The U.S. Coast Guard recommends not less than No. 14 U.S. ga. for tanks up to eighty gallons and 12 ga. up to 150 gallons; over this, $\frac{3}{16}''$. However, in commercial practice lighter sheet is generally used, but seldom less than 14 ga., 10 ga. for tanks up to about 300 gallons.

Diesel tanks are never galvanized, as the sulfuric acid in Diesel fuel will dissolve the zinc galvanizing. Instead they are generally of mild steel, welded. Deterioration is almost exclusively on the exterior, so if the metal is sandblasted and treated as recommended under steel boats, later in this book, they will last a very long time.

Aluminum tanks are advantageous where weight is a factor. They require no painting, but the right alloy should be used. The 5,000 series is acceptable (see Chapter 13). A heavier gauge is used, and for 200 gallons, about $\frac{5}{32}''$.

All connections must be isolated from copper or other fuel and vent lines by use of nylon, plastic, or non-magnetic connections at tank.

The copper tank is not recommended; stainless steel has a pitting problem. Monel, if the proper welding rod is used, is excellent. All tanks should be tested by screwing or otherwise fastening a standpipe of about eight feet and filling with water before installing in boat. This should be left for about twenty-four hours, and top openings plugged before installing in boat to avoid sawdust and dirt entering.

They must, of course, be well secured in place. Lugs are often welded to the

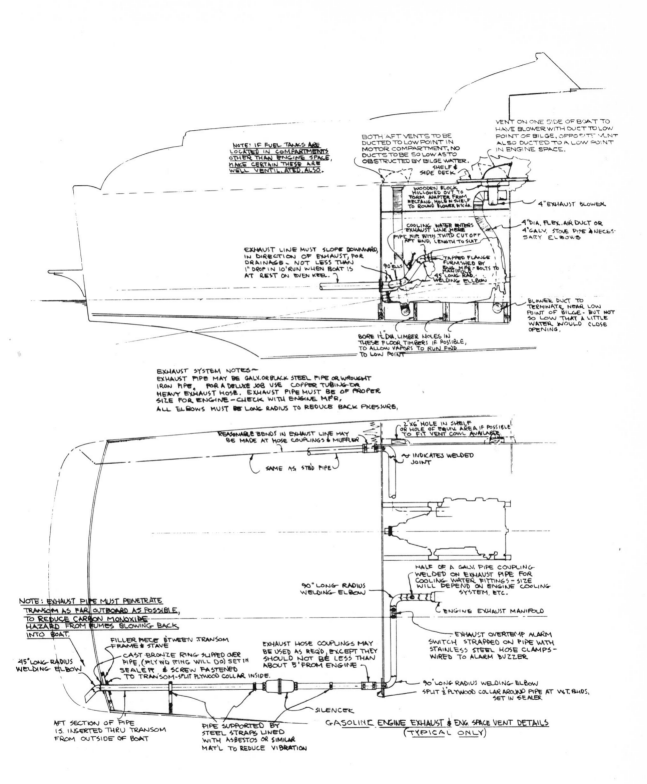

FIG. 98. Motor installation

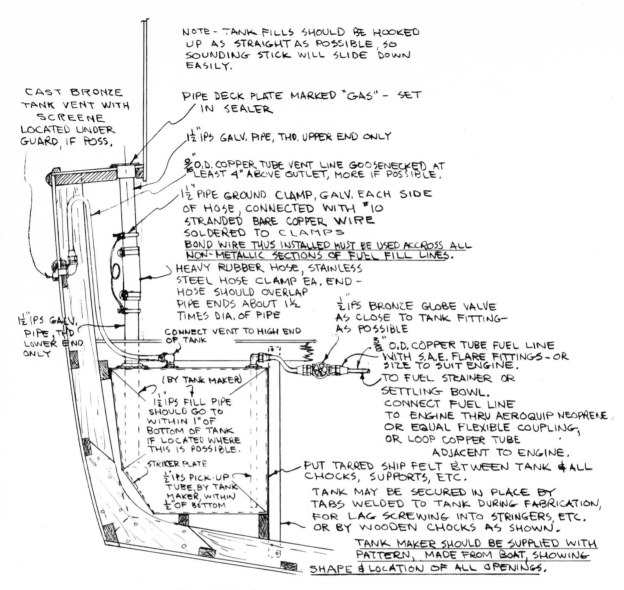

NOTE - TANK FILLS SHOULD BE HOOKED UP AS STRAIGHT AS POSSIBLE, SO SOUNDING STICK WILL SLIDE DOWN EASILY.

PIPE DECK PLATE MARKED "GAS" - SET IN SEALER

1½" IPS GALV. PIPE, THD. UPPER END ONLY

⁹⁄₁₆" O.D. COPPER TUBE VENT LINE GOOSENECKED AT LEAST 4" ABOVE OUTLET, MORE IF POSSIBLE.

1½" PIPE GROUND CLAMP, GALV. EACH SIDE OF HOSE, CONNECTED WITH #10 STRANDED BARE COPPER WIRE SOLDERED TO CLAMPS. BOND WIRE THUS INSTALLED MUST BE USED ACROSS ALL NON-METALLIC SECTIONS OF FUEL FILL LINES.

HEAVY RUBBER HOSE, STAINLESS STEEL HOSE CLAMP EA. END - HOSE SHOULD OVERLAP PIPE ENDS ABOUT 1½ TIMES DIA. OF PIPE

½" IPS BRONZE GLOBE VALVE AS CLOSE TO TANK FITTING AS POSSIBLE

CAST BRONZE TANK VENT WITH SCREENE LOCATED UNDER GUARD, IF POSS.

CONNECT VENT TO HIGH END OF TANK

1½" IPS GALV. PIPE, THD LOWER END ONLY

⅜" O.D. COPPER TUBE FUEL LINE WITH S.A.E. FLARE FITTINGS - OR SIZE TO SUIT ENGINE. TO FUEL STRAINER OR SETTLING BOWL. CONNECT FUEL LINE TO ENGINE THRU AEROQUIP NEOPRENE OR EQUAL FLEXIBLE COUPLING, OR LOOP COPPER TUBE ADJACENT TO ENGINE.

(BY TANK MAKER)

1½" IPS FILL PIPE SHOULD GO TO WITHIN 1" OF BOTTOM OF TANK IF LOCATED WHERE THIS IS POSSIBLE.

STRIKER PLATE

½" IPS PICK-UP TUBE, BY TANK MAKER WITHIN ½" OF BOTTOM

PUT TARRED SHIP FELT BETWEEN TANK & ALL CHOCKS, SUPPORTS, ETC.

TANK MAY BE SECURED IN PLACE BY TABS WELDED TO TANK DURING FABRICATION, FOR LAG SCREWING INTO STRINGERS, ETC. OR BY WOODEN CHOCKS AS SHOWN.

TANK MAKER SHOULD BE SUPPLIED WITH PATTERN, MADE FROM BOAT, SHOWING SHAPE & LOCATION OF ALL OPENINGS.

TANK NOTES -

1. TANKS SHOULD BE MADE ONLY BY AN EXPERIENCED TANK MAKER.

2. 14 GA. U.S.S. BLACK STEEL, HOT DIP GALV. AFTER FABRICATION MAKES A STRONG, ECONOMICAL TANK. (FOR NORMAL SIZE TANK)

3. ALL TANKS EXCEEDING 18" IN ANY HORIZONTAL DIMENSION, SHALL HAVE BAFFLE PLATES OF SAME MAT'L AS TANK WALLS, SPACED NOT MORE THAN 18" ON ℄.

4. ALL TANKS SHALL BE TESTED WITH A HEAD OF WATER 8 FT. ABOVE TOP OF TANK, FOR AT LEAST 6 HOURS.

TYPICAL GASOLINE FUEL TANK INSTALLATION

ALL GASOLINE FUEL SYSTEMS SHOULD BE IN ACCORDANCE WITH N.F.P.A. FIRE PROTECTION STANDARDS FOR MOTOR CRAFT, CHAPTER 3.

FIG. 99. Gasoline fuel tank installation

tank for this purpose. Tanks should not rest on a wide flat surface or platform where moisture will collect from condensation and perhaps destroy the tank.

Adequate baffles are necessary. The U. S. Coast Guard recommends thirty inches as a maximum free surface, less for thin gauge.

A settling pot with drain close to the supply outlet to motor is advantageous for Diesel installation, but settling pot with drain is not recommended for gasoline. Again, the U. S. Coast Guard stipulates all openings in gas tanks must be on top of the tank. This is not required at this writing for Diesel.

THE EXHAUST

On power boats the motor exhaust is usually well above the waterline, and the best place for the exhaust is out the stern. A decided drop is necessary where the pipe leaves the manifold to prevent water backing into the motor. Often two 45-degree elbows are used, and water should be placed in the line at the bottom of the drop.

Silencers are often placed quite close to the motor, though about the middle of the line is supposed to be the most effective location. Rubber silencers have largely replaced metal in wet exhausts, and rubber exhaust lines have some silencing effect. Should there be insufficient drop, the line must be goosenecked at the motor.

Sailboat exhausts are always a problem as the motor is usually below the waterline. To cope with this a special sailboat silencer is available. Figure 100 shows an installation with the exhaust out each side. This is not absolutely necessary, but when running under power and sail, as is sometimes done, the exhaust when buried will cause quite a pounding effect on the hull. Generally it is possible to exhaust out the stern, in which case the same principles apply, with a water-jacketed section carrying well up above the waterline and then aft. Copper tubing is probably the best material for exhaust pipes, except for Diesels, and water-jacketed bends can be made to almost any required shape; its cost, however, often makes its use prohibitive. Wrought iron or standard waterpipe can be water-jacketed by placing a large pipe over the smaller one and welding a flange at each end. An asbestos rope, also tape, is made that is very handy in insulating pipe, and the manufacturers recommend that the pipe first be wrapped, however, with expanded metal screen to provide air space between pipe and covering. A piece of exhaust hose should always be incorporated somewhere in the line close to the motor to provide flexibility. It also has a silencing effect.

As the Diesel's exhaust contains sulfuric acid, copper cannot be used for wet exhaust lines. Galvanized wrought-iron pipe is commonly used for this purpose; also there are several alloy tubings, made specially for the purpose. As the temperature of Diesel exhaust gases is much less than that of the gas engine, being about 800 to 950 degrees, the problem of cooling the exhaust

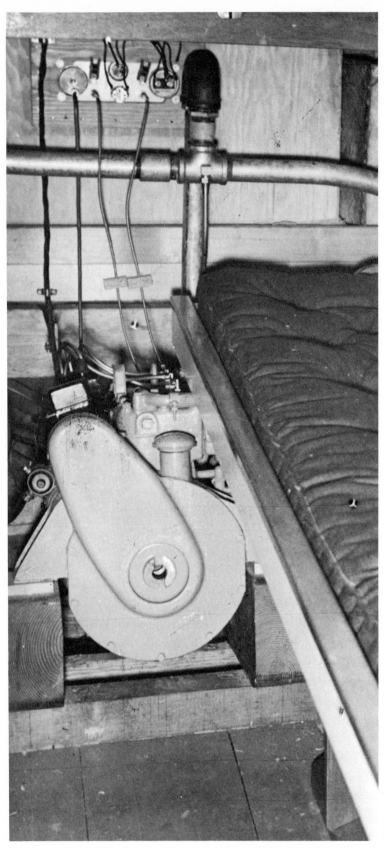

FIG. 100. Auxiliary engine with exhaust leading out both sides of a 28-foot sailboat

Photo by John Warren

line is not so difficult. In some cases where there is a low spot or pocket in the line also to reduce back pressure, only a small portion of the cooling water is put into it and the balance overboard. Neoprene exhaust hose is commonly used with good results and can be used to advantage where bends and twists are necessary.

A combination of steel pipe and rubber-hose connectors is good practice, and stainless-steel clamps should be used. For gasoline exhausts, light wall copper pipe or tubing is excellent.

A section of hose should always be used for gasoline engines also and as close to the engine as safety from burning permits; with dry exhaust, flexible stainless-steel tubing close to the exhaust manifold should be used.

Dry exhausts up through a stack have one advantage, as with fresh-water motor cooling one pump is dispensed with. They do, however, create a heat problem, and all woodwork should be kept well away from the hot pipe, which should be well insulated. The heat seems to build up, and what at first seems a satisfactory installation turns out on a long run to be inadequate.

MOTOR COOLING

Salt-water use almost dictates fresh-water cooling for extended use, as the salt clings to the walls of water passages and otherwise shortens the life of the motor.

This can be had through a heat exchanger on or adjacent to the motor or through tubes on the outside, generally called keel condensers.

There is not much difference in efficiency, as it has been proven that it takes as much power to force the cooling water through the heat exchanger as is expended by the heat exchanger tubes on the hull exterior. The latter are almost always copper and special fittings are commonly available for their installation. Be very sure, however, that Everdure bronze and not brass screws are used to fasten it on.

Steel and aluminum boats can often use the keel as a heat exchanger, and this is a common practice with work boats. A rough guide for temperate water is .20 square feet of cooling surface per H.P. More would be required for tropical water—at least twice this amount.

VENTILATING THE MOTOR COMPARTMENT

Where gasoline is used for motive power, it is imperative that some means of adequate ventilation be provided. Gasoline vapor is heavier than air and will lodge low in the bilge, ready to be set off by the first spark.

All safety organizations stress very strongly the necessity for adequate ventilation. At this writing, four vents are required for any engine-room compartment, the two forward ones to face aft and the aft ones forward. In addition to this, there must be an exhaust blower with sparkproof motor and with duct running to the low point of the bilge. All of the natural vents should also be ducted to a low point.

Safety experts recommend that tank fills not be closer than four feet to the nearest vent. However, this is not always possible. A more detailed list of requirements can be had from National Fire Protection Association, 60 Batterymarch Street, Boston, Massachusetts 02110.

Generally speaking, ventilation to a Diesel-engine compartment is dictated by the volume of air required for operation of the motor or motors. Roughly, at least .3 square inches per H.P. is recommended for four-cycle engines and .5 for two-cycle, and vents are often of the louver type. Where ducting is required, this should be increased.

In the interest of a cooler engine room, which means a little better motor performance and battery environment, additional air flow is all to the good.

Batteries when under charge discharge chlorine gas and if 32 volts or higher should be ventilated. Most adequately this is accomplished by enclosing the battery in a box with a vent leading directly outside; more often, however, it is done by merely ventilating the compartment.

WIRING

Wiring has become a complex subject with the introduction of electric heat and air conditioning, refrigeration, and the electric stove.

With care and large batteries, one can manage electrical refrigeration without an auxiliary generator, but it is not easy. The addition of any of the other above conveniences means the auxiliary generator and generally a converter, also shore connection when at dockside.

Such a complex installation should be engineered by a professional; however, a few basic practices will be helpful, particularly if the installation is fairly simple.

All wire should be not less than shown in the accompanying table (Fig. 101) as recommended by the United States Coast Guard.

Wiring should be plastic-covered, oil and waterproof multi-strand and fastened neatly in place by screw-fastened clips. This does not take long and is much superior to stapling.

Small, neat, low-cost circuit breakers are available and should be used instead of fuses. These can be mounted side by side in a very compact and neat installation. There is a rough rule that there should not be more than eight lights on any one circuit, and there should be an ample number of circuits so that if one piece of equipment shorts out, others will still be operative.

It is generally possible to have the same voltage for engine starting and ship service, and this is advisable. There should be two sets of batteries of equal

Total current on circuit, amperes	Length of conductor in feet from source of current to most distant fixture										
	10	15	20	25	30	35	40	45	50	55	60
6 volts, 2-wire—10 percent drop wire sizes (A.W.G.)											
5	14	14	14	12	12	12	10	10	10	10	8
10	14	12	10	10	8	8	8	8	6	6	6
15	12	10	8	8	8	6	6	6	4	4	4
20	10	8	8	6	6	6	4	4	4	4	3
25	10	8	6	6	4	4	4	4	3	3	2
12 volts, 2-wire—10 percent drop wire sizes (A.W.G.)											
5	14	14	14	14	14	14	14	14	12	12	12
10	14	14	14	12	12	12	10	10	10	10	8
15	14	14	12	10	10	10	8	8	8	8	8
20	12	12	10	10	8	8	8	8	6	6	6
25	10	10	10	8	8	8	6	6	6	6	4

FIG. 101.   Wire sizes, U.S. Coast Guard

size, with a double throw switch so that one set only is in operation at one time. Some prefer to use one set for ship service and the other for starting. However, this does not provide a stand-by for starting. In one instance where a dragging anchor made quick starting vital, the engine failed to start on one battery, and the stand-by probably saved the boat. Adequately heavy battery cable is very important, and distance to starter increases the gauge.

Batteries should be placed in a fiberglass or lead-lined box, though this is not always done. The purpose is to prevent any spill of the acid from damaging the hull. A cover over the batteries, preventing a short circuit by wrench or pliers, is advisable.

One circuit should be provided for the navigation lights, windshield swipes, compass light, etc., and small toggle or push-pull switches provided at steering position.

Wiring should be accessible where possible, and the space behind curtain valance board (see Fig. 73) forms a handy wireway.

12/
SPARS AND
SPAR MAKING

COMPETITION IS DOUBTLESS the major driving force behind most improvement, and nowhere is it keener than in the designing and handling of the racing or cruising sailboat. The simple solid pole has been replaced by the aluminum, and the hollow spruce spar of various shapes and sections with a rather complicated system of spreaders, struts, and staying.

Aerodynamics has proven a certain merit in the streamlining of masts, and this, combined with the fact that the spar's greatest strength is required in the fore and aft direction, is the justification for the many shapes developed by designers.

Figure 103 shows a large number of spar shapes, each one adapted to its particular use or possessing some merit. Number One is the simple two-piece round spar, and though ideal for spinnaker boom and for some other purposes, it does not have the best distribution of material for masts.

Number Two is the same with one corner left on in finishing it up from square to round. This is an improvement over the first figure in that it possesses greater fore and aft strength, in which direction the greatest strain occurs. No batten is required for the track in this spar.

Number Three is a box spar whose chief advantage is ease of construction and the fact that less spruce is required and the thinner material can be more easily obtained. This spar is widely used and often seen on small racing, "one design," craft as well as larger boats.

Number Four is a true streamlined spar. This and Number Seven, as well as the mast shown in Fig. 106, approach the ideal in distribution of material in that the greatest stiffness is in the fore and aft direction and it also offers less resistance in going to windward. The stock gooseneck, bands, etc., will not, however, fit these shapes except perhaps that with long bolts joining the two halves of the band on outside of mast they might be adapted to Number Seven.

FIG. 102. Boat under sail

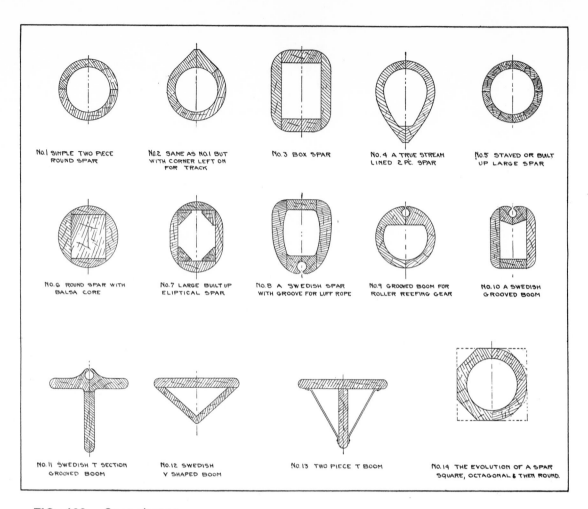

FIG. 103. Spar shapes

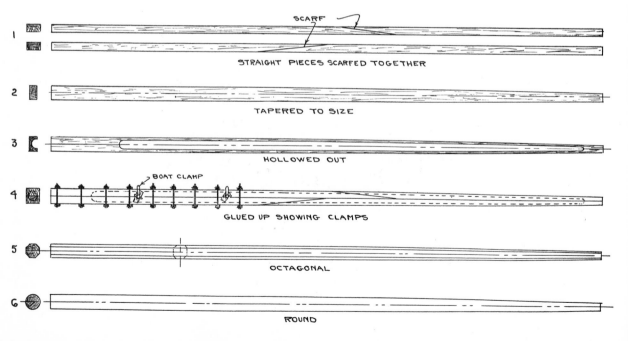

FIG. 104. The evolution of a spar

DIMENSIONS OF SOLID SPRUCE SPARS

	TOP OF DECK				¢ OF SHEAVE
CAT BOAT - NO SHROUDS	DIA = .016 OF LENGTH	.94 D.	.85 D.	.73 D.	.58 D.	.42 D.
CRUISING BOAT - STAYED MASTS	DIA = .0120"	1.100 D.	.98 D.	.95 D.	.85 D.	1.50 D.

MAST DIAMETERS FOR MARCONI OR JIB HEADED RIG

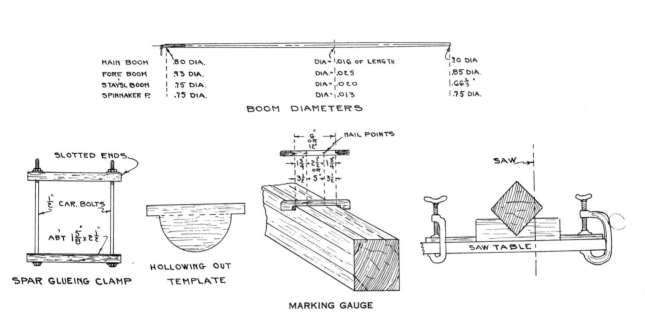

MAIN BOOM	.80 DIA.	DIA = .016 OF LENGTH	.70 DIA.
FORE BOOM	.93 DIA.	DIA = .025	1.85 DIA.
STAYSL BOOM	.75 DIA.	DIA = .020	1.66⅔ "
SPINNAKER P.	.75 DIA.	DIA = .013	1.75 DIA.

BOOM DIAMETERS

SLOTTED ENDS

½" CAR. BOLTS

ABT 1⅝" x 2½"

SPAR GLUEING CLAMP

HOLLOWING OUT TEMPLATE

NAIL POINTS

6 OR 12"

1¾ 2½ 1¾ OR 3½ 5 3½

MARKING GAUGE

SAW

SAW TABLE

FIG. 105. Spar diameters and implements

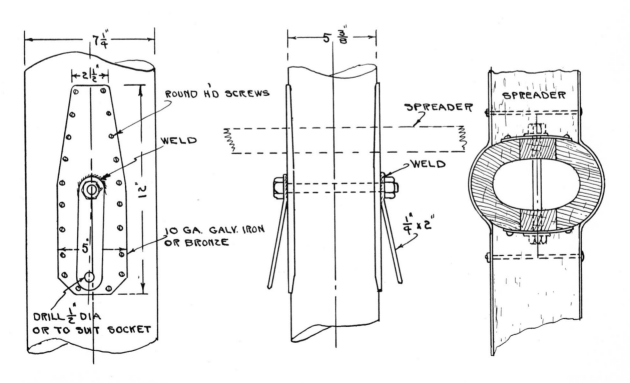

7¼"

2½"

ROUND HD SCREWS

WELD

21"

5"

10 GA. GALV. IRON OR BRONZE

DRILL ½" DIA OR TO SUIT SOCKET

5⅜"

SPREADER

WELD

¼" x 2"

SPREADER

FIG. 106. Tang fittings

Number Five is sometimes used on very large spars, as also is Seven. Eight has a groove for the luff rope instead of the conventional track. Number Nine is a section of a boom used in connection with a roller reefing gear, and in this case the spar is not tapered but carries its full diameter from end to end.

The balance of the figures are various shapes of booms—Number Ten a very neat box spar, Twelve an effective use of materials. The T section of Number Eleven must, however, entail a great deal of labor and is quite a departure from the orthodox. The Swedes, with their square meter classes, have developed the smaller racing craft to a very high degree of perfection, and it is from them that most of these odd-shaped spars are derived.

The large cup-defenders presented the last word in large mast construction, and here the designers turned from wood to metal. The *Endeavor*'s spar was of high tensile steel, built of plates electrically welded and strengthened against collapse by light diaphragms as in a rod of bamboo, and this mast was 168 feet long. *Rainbow*'s mast was of duraluminum and was pear-shaped, similar to Number Four. By careful designing a saving was made of between 600 and 900 pounds over the fittings required for a wooden mast. In 1930 a minimum weight limit was placed on cup-racers' masts.

HOLLOW SPARS

Most masts are now made hollow, the additional cost being justified by the great saving in weight. To illustrate this we will take a four-inch spruce spar of solid section which will weigh 2.88 pounds per foot. By increasing the diameter to but 4½″ and hollowing out the center until it weighs but 1.75 pounds, it will still be equally as strong as the solid piece. The mast of a thirty-six-foot sloop will probably extend fifty feet above the boat's center of gravity and its keel about five feet below. Every pound saved at the top of the mast will be equivalent to the addition of about ten pounds of outside ballast. Eliminating this additional ballast (multiplied many times) plus the weight saved in the spar means less displacement and less wetted surface, which, all summed up, means more speed.

Most spars of any size and all hollow ones are glued up of two or more pieces, and Sitka spruce is the prime spar-making material, being the lightest wood for its strength on the North American continent. In addition to this it does not check, takes glue exceedingly well, and finishes up nicely under varnish. The development of glue to the point where it can be implicitly relied upon has of course made possible the hollow spar. The writer has seen spars fail for various reasons, but never through any fault of the glue. They should be solid at deck (if wedged), at gooseneck band, and at spreaders. This is accomplished by fillers.

The extruded aluminum spar has largely replaced the wooden one. Where labor is involved, it is less costly, though the home builder can make his own of wood and effect quite a saving. The properly proportioned wood mast seems able to take a bending stress better than its metal counterpart. At least, in a hard blow that broke eleven masts in a fairly large race turnout, none of the wooden masts failed, even though some lost forestays, etc.

MAST STRESSES

Contrary to the general impression, the principal stress on a mast is compression, and if properly stayed the bending stress is comparatively slight. Masts have often been stepped on deck. Uffa Fox is quite an exponent of this method, his theory being that if the standing rigging carries away and the spar goes overside there is less likelihood of breakage. Another departure from the orthodox is stepping the mast below but not wedging it at the deck; the hole is cut to allow about an inch of play all around and a canvas skirt fitted for watertightness. As it is comparatively easy to stay a mast thwartship and difficult to stay it fore and aft, the elliptical or similarly shaped mast offers the most efficient distribution of material. Numbers Three, Four, and Seven are examples. They are also made up as in Number One with a filler piece between the walls of the two halves.

FIG. 107. Hollow mast glued up. Note bolt clamps in middle section. *Photo by Ray Krantz*

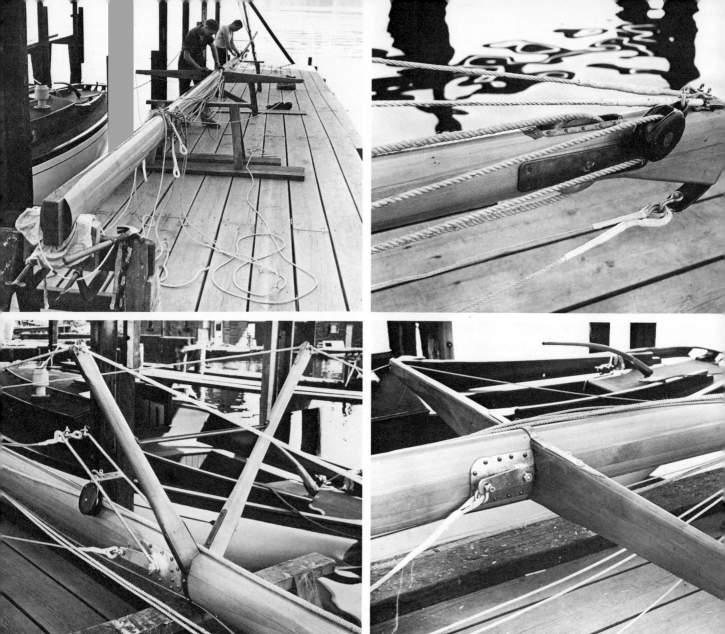

FIG. 108. (Upper left) Attaching spreader to mast

Photo by Ray Krantz

FIG. 109. (Upper right) Masthead showing strut stays on one side and back stay and boom lift on other. The block is temporary.

Photo by Ray Krantz

FIG. 110. (Lower left) V-strut and bail for forestay, and jib halyard block

Photo by Ray Krantz

FIG. 111. (Lower right) Main spreader showing tang fittings. The shroud, however, is generally attached to a tang with socket fitting instead of shackle.

Photo by Ray Krantz

SPAR DIMENSIONS

The designer generally shows on the sail plan the proper spar dimensions; if not, the table on page 123 will give these dimensions. For hollow spars the wall thickness is not always given, and sometimes it is found desirable to replace a solid stick with a hollow one, which will necessitate a slightly larger diameter. A rough and thoroughly tried formula for the latter is to increase the diameter by 10 percent. As to wall thickness, I have found that a wall thickness of 15 percent of diameter for each wall is a safe minimum. The Norwegian Skerry rule states that the walls must not be less than one-fifth the mast's diameter at two-thirds the distance from deck to the fastening point of the lower shrouds. The ocean racer *Nina*'s mast has a wall thickness of 14 percent and a lot of hard driving has proven it to be of ample strength. In the average cruising boat there is no object in going to extremes, and I would make each wall not less than 15 percent of diameter, and a little thicker will not add much to the weight and will provide a factor of safety.

Given the sail plan, the aluminum spar maker will engineer the required extrusion size and furnish the mast complete with tangs, etc.

MAKING A MAST

We will follow through here the construction of a hollow mast made up of two pieces to the cross-section, and the same principles will apply to all hollow or solid spars. Presuming the stick is too long to be obtained in one length, the first operation will be to glue the pieces up into two halves the desired length. A shim end scarf is used and it should not be shorter than six times the diameter of the spar. The sticks should first be jointed on the surfaces that will be joined together when glued up and the scarfs carefully fitted. It is customary to break joints so that scarfs do not come together, though this makes little difference, and there are many spars with scarfs opposite.

Use, of course, waterproof glue and mix it according to directions. A very necessary requisite is the application of plenty of pressure, so do not spare the clamps. A chalkline is stretched down the center to line up the pieces, and after the glue has set the scarfed portion is jointed or planed smooth. The taper is then laid off and the stick sawed to shape. On account of the extreme length of the finished stick it is often advisable to saw the taper before scarfing the two pieces together.

Now comes the hollowing out. If a shaper is available it is done with this tool, but if not it must be done by hand, using a gouge and finishing up with a round plane. Several templates similar to the one shown are made and the wood whittled out to fit. It is customary to leave the butt solid up to above the deck or above the gooseneck band, also the top down past the sheave. The inside of the spar is given a coat of shellac or other wood sealer. The plain box spar, Number Three, Fig. 103, is really the most practical shape and the most widely used. The same scarfing and tapering is used and with flat, not edge, scarfs.

We are now ready to glue up the two halves, and as this requires a very large number of clamps, it is seldom that such a quantity is available even in the boat shop. Special and inexpensive clamps are made for the purpose, using two carriage bolts about one-half-inch diameter and two cross-pieces with slotted ends for each clamp. An arrangement can often be made whereby the bolts may be returned at a small discount. Clamps should be spaced about a foot or fifteen inches apart, and it is best to place all the clamps on the spar in their proper position and with nuts loosely in place before actually glueing up. These are then removed and placed in order opposite their position on the spar.

A long stick will require three or four hands to set up the clamps before the glue has time to set. Every six feet or so a boat clamp is placed to line up the edges and to relieve the bulging stress of the other clamps; place newspaper under the blocks. Forty-eight hours at least should be allowed for glue to dry.

We now have a square or rectangular tapered stick, and the next step is to shape it to octagonal for round mast or boom. A scribing tool is made for laying this out, as shown, from a piece of hardwood and two nails. A notched holding piece can be placed on the band-saw table and the corners accurately sawed. As this piece will tend to slide into the saw, a thin piece must be clamped to the table against which the piece will slide. A simple job of streamlining may be had by leaving one corner on as shown in Number Two. This is flattened off to suit the track.

The spar is now smoothed up with spar knife (draw knife) and plane, finishing up with a hollow or spar plane if one is available. In sanding the stick a piece of cork or soft wood is hollowed to the greatest diameter and used as a sanding block. Use coarse sandpaper on pipe or can to hollow the block.

In laying out all spars, particularly booms, some consideration should be given to the size of fittings available, at least for the gooseneck band. Number Nine in the spar sections (Fig. 103) shows how a boom for roller reefing is made. The forward end must be flattened off or the slot widened sufficiently to enter the rope in the foot of the sail, and the aft end must be flattened to install clew outhaul. There are several types of roller reefing gear, but the boom is usually made the same diameter its full length.

SPREADERS AND STRUT DETAILS

Shown in Figs. 106 and 113 are details of some spreaders, struts, and fittings commonly found on most spar-making jobs. Dimensions are shown and smaller or larger fittings may be made in proportion.

There are two types of spreaders in general use—the solid spruce and the

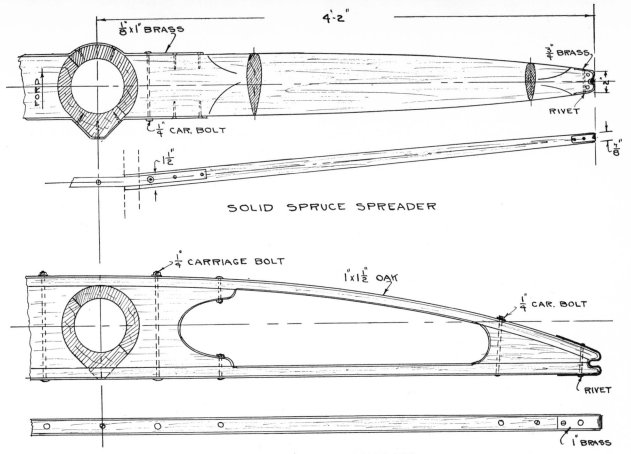

FIG. 112. Spreaders

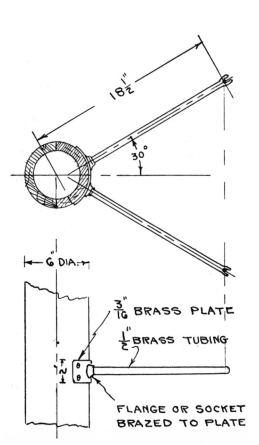

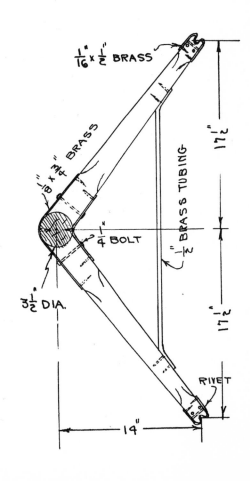

FIG. 113. V-strut

built-up type; both of these are shown in Fig. 112. Spreaders are of course subject to end pressure only and may be considered as struts, and their exact dimensions can thus be calculated, but except in rare instances this is seldom done. The proportions shown are about right and have stood the test of several years' hard sailing. The two holes in the tip are used for lashing to the stay; spreader lifts are also often employed to support the outboard ends. The built-up spreader is perhaps stronger than the solid type but is heavier and also offers more wind resistance. It is suitable for heavy cruising boats and where the shroud leads well aft, requiring a spreader with ends or tips aft. Where possible the spreader should bisect the angle of the shroud; otherwise there is a bending stress set up, but this is of course not possible with the built-up type. As the mainsail when square off exerts quite a pressure against the spreader, these are often made to hinge forward. Sometimes this pressure is actually enough to twist the mast; however, the majority are fixed, including most of the ocean racers which encounter the most severe conditions.

Figure 113 shows details of two V or jumper stay struts used so often on the forward side of the mast to take the pull of the jib or says'l stay. One is made of metal tubing fitted into flanges brazed to the curved plate; the other is of wood and has a wider spread to serve also as a spreader.

It is not intended here to cover the rigging of the boat, but tang fittings have replaced spliced loops around the mast. These fittings are neater, lighter, and greatly simplify the removal of the mast for winter storage. Figure 106 shows tang fittings at the lower spreaders on the mast of a thirty-four-foot cutter. For smaller or larger spars, weights and dimensions would be proportional.

Use, of course, stainless-steel standing rigging, seven-strand. The turn buckles should be of larger diameter than the wire and of the same breaking strength.

Wire halliards do not stretch, but they necessitate halliard winches unless married to a fabric line permitting use of a gypsy head winch and a cleat.

Blocks for the Genoa sheet should be on a track on the rail so they can be adjusted, and the flat track for traveler is more in the way than the rod type.

The use of tang fittings eliminates practically all splicing, and sockets are used instead. These are of two types, one in which the wire is splayed out and held in place by pouring in melted zinc, the other in which a cone is forced into the center of the strands, wedging the wire tightly in place. If the labor of splicing is considered, these fittings cost no more than splicing and serving the loops around the mast or splicing the lower ends for the thimbles and are much neater.

All the spar and spar-fittings photos shown here are of the mast of a thirty-four-foot cutter. This spruce mast is hollow, of an overall length of fifty-one-feet, is of oval section 5¼″ x 7½″ at deck and 2⅞″ x 3⅞″ at the top. The hollow starts just above the boom bands where the walls are 1¼″ thick and ends just below the sheave where they are ⅞″. As the photos show, this stick is of a four-piece section, as in Fig. 106, which is a detail of this spar.

As the glueing-up illustration shows, there were not enough boat clamps to do the job, so bolt clamps were resorted to. Note the numerous supports under the stick. The first layer was shimmed and wedged perfectly straight and secured in place before glueing up. Figure 106 shows dimensions of lower tangs at main spreaders and detail of their assembly.

In Fig. 110 showing the V strut, it will be noted that the halyard block is to one side, and another block will be shackled in the hole shown, as there are twin headstays. With this arrangement a Genoa, for instance, may be run up while the working job is still in place.

FIG. 114. Rigging a 28-foot ketch

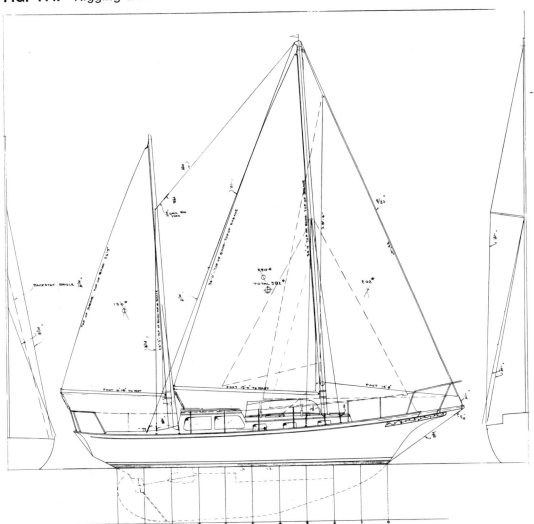

The slot for the masthead sheave is lined on the sides with thin sheet copper and the bottom is sheathed with lead to keep water from rotting the mast. Eye splices are shown in the rigging wire, but socket fittings fit in better and are simpler and lighter.

There are a large number of firms supplying fittings and blocks for sailboats. The builder should obtain one or more catalogues and turn out the spars to suit the hardware.

13 THE ALUMINUM BOAT

ALUMINUM HAS BEEN IN USE in marine construction in a limited way since 1890 when a naphtha launch, the *Zephyr,* was built in Zurich, Switzerland. It did not, however, come into what might be termed general use until the advent of heliarc welding.

Mild steel used in boat and ship building ranges in ultimate strength from 58,000# to 71,000#, and the 5,000 series aluminum most commonly used for this purpose ranges from 31,000# to 63,000#. To compensate for this the aluminum sheet or shape must of course be thicker. A rather rough compensating factor is 1.3 for plates and 1.5 for shapes such as angles and tees.

FIG. 115. 42-foot aluminum cruiser. Note motor vents in hull. *Photo by Ray Krantz*

Aluminum weighs about 156# per cubic foot and steel 460#. However, as the metal must be thicker, the ultimate weight ratio is about 50 percent. This applies to the structure only, and as motor, equipment, etc., will weigh the same, the weight saving on the completed boat will probably be in the neighborhood of 15 percent, actually about the same as a wood boat of light construction.

The aluminum hull became practical for salt-water use with the advent of alloys that are resistant to corrosion in sea water.

Aluminum has some advantages over steel besides being much lighter. If properly protected from electrolysis, it does not corrode; in fact many aluminum boats, and some fairly large ones, are not painted at all. A thin film of aluminum oxide forms on the surface and inhibits further corrosion.

It is pleasant to work, as it can be readily sawed as well as burned, and of course large plates are easier to handle. Disadvantages are higher first cost, plus a certain precaution to protect the metal from electrolytic action, also aluminum distorts more readily than steel.

SUITABLE ALLOYS

Aluminum alloys are designated by an Aluminum Association number, and all manufacturers comply with these standard designations. The 5000 series is suitable for marine application, as well as Number 6061. Most widely used are Numbers 5083-H34 and H113, and Numbers 5086-H34 and H32; 5052 in the quarter hard, or H.32. Aluminum is alloyed with magnesium and manganese in the 5000 series.

The H numbers designate hardness, as you have probably surmised. Welding metal is also designated by number, and the builder should use that recommended by the particular manufacturer of plate or shape.

Following is what one of our largest aluminum firms has to say about the various alloys mentioned above:

5052—High-strength alloy is tough, yet easily worked, and is suitable for general marine use.

5083—Widely used for seagoing boats of larger sizes, but not as easily worked as Number 5052; it is very tough and used on some naval vessels as armor plate.

5086—Similar to 5083, has good forming characteristics, and a specified as most desirable by U. S. Bureau of Ships for ship construction and repair.

6061—Extensively used for framing of boats, but not for hull plating if boat is for salt-water use. All the aluminum alloys are subject to galvanic action, or electrolysis, when in contact with steel or bronze. This will occur even though the metals are not submerged in sea water. Aluminum must be insulated from contact with other metals. There must be a plastic, neoprene, nylon, or similar

FIG. 116. Aluminum hull showing plating **FIG. 117.** Bow framing of 42-foot power boat

Photo by Maarten and Strode

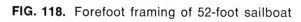

FIG. 118. Forefoot framing of 52-foot sailboat **FIG. 119.** Frame of 52-foot sailboat

connection between any tank spud or fitting and copper or other metal fuel or water lines. Plastic water lines are, of course, ideal.

The higher the hardness number, the smaller the bending radius for the plate. As an example, 5086-32 ⅛″ plate can be bent to a radius of ⅛″ to ¼″ whereas with H34 the radius is ³⁄₁₆″ to ⁵⁄₁₆″. There is only a small difference in strength, the higher number having somewhat higher yield strength.

Number 6061 is a somewhat stronger alloy but suffers a much greater loss of strength at the weld.

Rudder stocks and propeller shafts should be stainless-steel of the proper alloy. Number 316 is suitable for rudder stocks, and there are several trade-name stainless-steel propeller shafts whose alloy is compatible with aluminum.

WELDING

Welding is most practical using the inert gas-shielded metallic arc, termed MIG, process. The shielding should be argon or a mixture of argon and helium. Twenty-five percent argon and 75 percent helium seems to work best for heavy sections.

It is necessary to place tack welds closer together than with steel to keep the joint from opening during welding. Small tacks as close as three inches apart may be required for light metal.

Before welding it is essential to clean the prepared edges with solvent if there is any likelihood of oil or grease on the edges. Where oxide film may be heavy, as with material exposed to outdoor storage for any length of time, it should be cleaned by wire brushing and preferably by hand. This is not effective unless grease has been previously removed. Power cleaning should be done lightly to prevent surface entrapment of contaminants.

The weld area should be protected from the wind and its accompanying dirt by portable windshields. There is now available a special tape for backing up the weld.

Shown is a typical butt joint. The gap should not exceed ⅛″. From ½″ and above, one of the edges had best be beveled.

T joints, such as bulkheads to shell, should be beveled and welded on both sides and the fillet dimension T should slightly exceed the thickness of the bulkhead or other member in this position. Rough edges must be smoothed, and if a file is used, it should have about ten teeth per inch.

WELDING SEQUENCE—See Chapter 14. As with the plywood boat, a conically developed bow—that is, from chine down—enables the builder to use a large plate without splitting for the underbody bow section. This is not, generally at least, done with larger hulls, say thirty-two feet and up, and it produces a rather full, though also a strong, section.

LOCATION OF PLATE WELDS—Wherever feasible these should be at or close to a longitudinal, stiffener, or other support. Where the joining surfaces

FIG. 120. Aluminum sailboat set up upside down showing t-bar stringers let into frames, and framing for hollow ballast keel

or edges, bulkheads, etc., are in the very bottom of the bilge, the welds should be continuous so as to keep out contaminated bilge water. A metal boat should, however, have a dry bilge except perhaps in the compartment where the stuffing box is situated.

Aluminum seems somewhat prone to failure from vibration. This sometimes occurs over the propeller or propellers, and a doubler or somewhat heavier plate is often used to remedy this.

CUTTING ALUMINUM—This can be done with band saw, saber saw, skil saw or router, and large shops use nibblers. The band saw, or other saw used, must be suitable for aluminum, with teeth suitably spaced. Some authorities state that square-edge cuts are satisfactory for welds up to ¾₆"; thicker than this, the plate should be beveled. In Kaiser's "Welding," however, ½" plate can be butt-welded satisfactorily (Fig. 121). Beveling can be done by a router. Single-pass welds are satisfactory, provided good weld penetration is had.

Doubler plates, openings in bulkheads, etc., should not have square corners but should be radiused.

WORKING THE PLATES—This is done in a similar manner as described in "The Steel Boat," though a rubber mallet may be quite useful. Moderate heating by use of a blow torch is helpful on a difficult bend, but a 500-degree F. temperature crayon should be used to avoid overheating.

It is general practice as with the steel hull to insulate the hull interior above the cabin floor line. A sprayed-on coat makes the nicest job, as it covers frames and longitudinals. Asbestos is often used; also there are several trade-name materials whose basic content seems to be asphalt and ground cork sprayed on about ¼" thick. When dry, they are very slow-burning, not a fire hazard. Then there are the sprayed on styrofoam-like materials coating the steel to one inch thickness or more.

The space between ceiling and hull and the overhead can be treated as described in "The Steel Boat."

PAINTING

Paint adheres very well to aluminum, provided the surface is clean, and, unlike steel, there is no mill scale to contend with. However, the surface should have some preparation either by cleaning with a detergent or soap or use of a commercial non-etch alkaline cleaner made for aluminum.

Cleaning with a stainless-steel wire brush or stainless-steel wool has the added advantage of roughing the surface and improving the adherence of the paint.

As with all boat-building materials, the paint manufacturers each have their own painting schedule, and this should be followed. It is quite customary to plaster the minor hollows as with a steel hull, and there are special materials

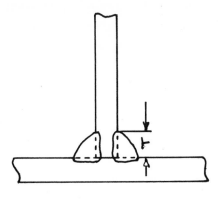

T JOINT

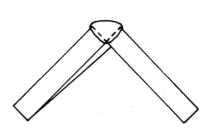

CORNER JOINT

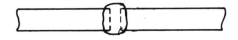

BUTT JOINT

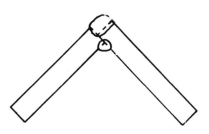

CORNER JOINT

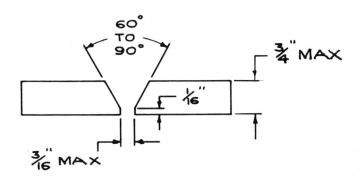

SINGLE V JOINT ¾" MAX THICKNESS

FIG. 121. Various welds

made for this purpose. They are applied by trowel and sanded smooth when dry.

The paint must be compatible with aluminum, and those containing mercury must not be used. Anti-fouling copper paints must have an insulating coat or coats applied to the hull first. There are some anti-fouling paints that are compatible with aluminum.

A very efficient way to apply paint is with one man applying it with a roller, followed closely by another with a brush to smooth it out.

I am indebted to the Aluminum Company of America for permission to quote from their publications. This company, also Reynolds Aluminum and Kaiser Aluminum, all have publications on the fabrication of this metal, some pertaining to its use in boats, which are generally obtainable for the asking if one is seriously interested.

14/ THE STEEL BOAT

TIME WAS, and not so very far in the past, that only a well-equipped shipyard was capable of building a steel boat. This was the day of the riveted hull. Plate shears, bending slab and furnace, plate punch, riveting gun, and other costly equipment were required.

The electric arc welder and the acetylene torch have changed this and revolutionized the craft, bringing it within the means and skill of most good mechanics familiar with welding technique.

Steel has largely replaced wood in the towboat industry and in the fishing fleet for boats over about forty-two feet in length. A few firms are building pleasure boats as small as thirty feet, but in this field its unavoidable weight handicap limits its wider use in boats much less than seventy feet. There is however, a point somewhere near 100 feet when steel even becomes lighter than wood.

The steel hull possesses several advantages. Fuel and water tanks can be built integral with the hull, thus saving space and permitting, where desired, a much larger fuel and water tankage.

Properly treated, there is little rust and of course no teredo or worm hazard and no dry rot. It does require more insulation in living quarters; also the metal must be properly treated, either before placing in the boat by "wheelebrating" or other preassembly methods, or by sandblasting, which is generally done after erecting and when all welding is completed. Prior treatment is much less expensive and, when properly done and immediately followed by a protective priming coat, is very effective.

All the above is necessary to remove the mill scale which prevents the paint from adhering properly to the metal and thus followed inevitably by rust.

Steel is often claimed as having such disadvantages over wood as being noisier as well as colder in winter and hotter in summer. The latter can be overcome with adequate insulation. Sweating is another problem, but this can be combated by one of the direct-contact insulating coats, generally a mixture of

FIG. 122. Longitudinally framed, 50-foot, steel troller-cruiser

Photo by Deines Studio

FIG. 123. Stern of double chine, longitudinally framed, 50-foot, steel troller-cruiser

Photo by Deines Studio

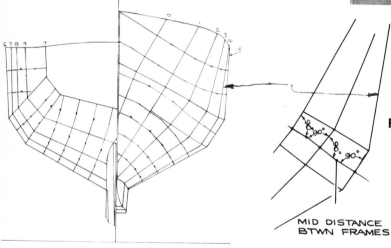

MID DISTANCE
BTWN FRAMES

FIG. 124. Laying out for longitudinal stringers

FIG. 125. Plating 50-foot, steel troller showing dogs welded to lower plate for forcing top plate home. Forebody below chine was not conically developed, hence plating is in three strakes.

Photo by Deines Studio

asphalt and cork to a thickness of about ¼″, also a sprayed-on styrofoam-like coating. (See Chapter 13.)

Common mild steel is generally used (trade designation, A 36). There is some advantage to special steels, some of them copper born and not only stronger but less subject to rust. They are also harder to work and for this reason avoided by some builders. Because they are stiffer, a lighter gauge can be used on decks and sides of deck erections. The U. S. Coast Guard specifies American Bureau of Shipping-inspected steel for boats carrying passengers or freight for hire, but this would seem a superfluous requirement for pleasure or commercial building.

Often in pleasure boats, to save weight, the hull only is steel, with plywood bulkheads bolted to web frames and with plywood decks, either fiberglassed or teak-covered. Pleasure boats have wood superstructures, but commercial craft prefer steel as it is tighter and generally weight is not a major consideration.

The metal boat can utilize the keel as a "keel condenser," as it is called, for removing the heat from engine-cooling water. This is the simplest of all heat exchangers and, with dry exhaust, requires no additional pump as does the engine with integral heat exchanger.

Generally, the classification societies have given the small steel boat scant consideration compared to the elaborate rules for constructing ships. However, there is sufficient data to specify thickness of plating, bulkheads, stiffeners, etc., and I think most architects try to comply with these recommendations.

Lofting a steel boat is, of course, little different from a wood hull. Common practice does not deduct for thickness of shell plating, as one would do with wood planking. This adds a small amount to displacement, however, as boats in general are heavier than calculated; it is considered a sort of bonus. There is a real advantage in conical development of bow section below chine in smaller boats. (See "Plywood Construction.")

Careful lofting is more important than with a wood hull and will be time well spent. A more elaborate or thorough job is also necessary, as bulkheads with stiffeners in place should be built on the floor. Waterlines, diagonals, and buttocks should be faired up carefully, particularly if the hull is transverse framed with the frames closely spaced.

With a longitudinally framed boat it is possible to cut the notches for the stringers in the bulkheads and web frames before erecting them, as shown in the illustration. T-bar bends much easier than does an angle, as it does not have the angle's tendency to upset at the hard bends. However, angles are more often used, being more readily available.

Erecting the hull upside down is a real advantage, particularly for welding. This is generally feasible with a small boat only, though if the builder feels the added labor and expense is warranted, a turning wheel will make this possible on a fairly large boat. It has been done on 100-footers, and two wheels can of course be employed. Often a smaller boat—say, forty to forty-five feet—is dragged out of the shop and turned by a crane and then pulled back in again.

In the not too distant past, almost all steel boats were round-bilge. This required rolling some of the plates—a vanishing skill. Today the hulls are either V-bottom with one chine, or double chine. Compound bends are thus almost eliminated, and hull plates are pulled in place with "come alongs," clamps, and wedges. Hard bends on railings, etc., are heated with a torch and pulled in place at the same time, and it is amazing how neatly this can be done.

A considerable hollow flare forward, so enhancing to appearance, can be handled by cutting the plate into strips perhaps about sixteen inches wide and plating the area diagonally or vertically.

In erecting the boat right side up, the stem is held in place by two light angles tack welded in place. Bilge shores where needed are likewise treated, as is internal bracing where required.

Web frames, generally plate with flange on the inside edge, had best be flanged in a brake, provided of course that the inboard edge is straight. If no brake is available, the flange can be welded in place. Intermittent welding on the inside corner is considered adequate.

FIG. 126. Plate in place ready to clamp and wedge to frames and longitudinals of 50-foot steel troller-cruiser   *Photo by Deines Studio*

Welding seems almost the key to a good boat. On it largely depends the fairness of the hull and its strength. The U.S. Coast Guard places so much importance on this that all welders on passenger boats must be certified by their organization.

Distortion is the bugaboo. I recall a forty-five-foot V-bottom cruiser with one edge of the transom about four inches higher than the other, caused by improper procedure. One must not, however, become too alarmed with a few humps or hollows in shell or deck plating, as this occurs with the most experienced builders. These can be taken out by procedures covered later in these pages.

A few small hollows will almost always remain, and it is common practice where a smooth appearance is required to "plaster" the hull exterior, as it is termed. The plaster is a commercial product applied with a trowel, sanded, and smoothed off much as is done in body work with an automobile.

The entire hull is first tack-welded together, and at this point it almost always looks fair to the eye. Welding should start in the middle of the boat, and the welder should move from side to side and work both ways from the midships.

FIG. 127. Construction sections of 50-foot ketch longitudinally framed showing double chine

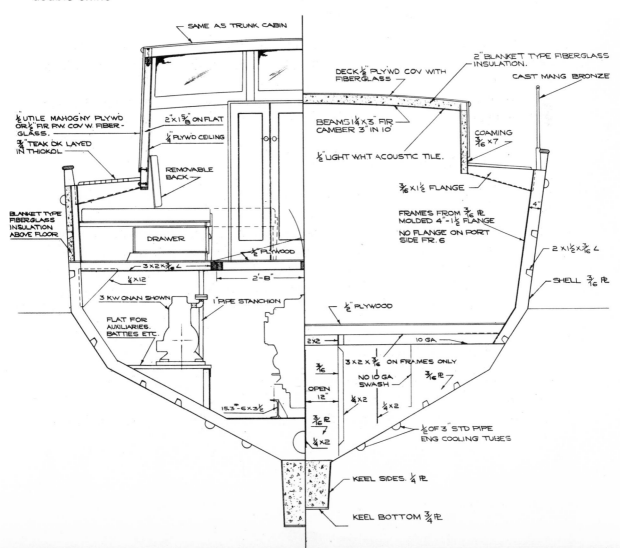

The American Bureau of Shipping has evolved a welding schedule. This is for fairly large craft and heavy plating, so for lighter material the same proportion of weld and skip should be retained, as has been done in the accompanying table for 10 gauge and $\frac{3}{16}''$ plate.

Welding should be preceded by making sure the edges and surfaces are clean and free of oil, paint, scale, and dirt. Shown are a typical chain-type weld and a staggered weld.

There are other stipulations in the Bureau rules, but they would seem to apply to ships rather than boats.

Ship Design and Construction, published by the Society of Naval Architects and Marine Engineers, contains some very pertinent information, though again its principal concern is the large ship. Much of the following is based on this book, edited by Mr. Amelio M. D. Archangelo.

It does not recommend that bulwarks be welded directly to the hull, as the bulwark cap then becomes the extreme fiber in the structure. This, nevertheless, is common practice in the boat field.

The serrations in the bilge keel (as shown in the photo) provide a resilient connection to the hull.

WELDING ELECTRODES

A welding electrode is a core of rod with a covering to protect the arc and molten metal from the atmosphere and to impart certain metallurgical properties to the weld.

As most have been designed for a particular use, it is advisable that your steel supplier specify the proper rod.

DISTORTION

As the weld metal contracts upon cooling in the order of about 2 percent in all directions, it pulls the plate with it.

There is another factor called the upsetting factor. The book states that it is more difficult to explain, but, very much oversimplified, it is about as follows: A small and single section of plate confined at opposite edges expands only on the unrestrained edges, but when it cools it tries to shrink in all directions, pulling together the two restraining plates.

WELDING SEQUENCE

Ship Design and Construction states that the basic principle of welding sequence is shown in the following figure from the book.

In the accompanying figure the butt is welded first; in this sequence the

FIG. 128. Spacing of welds and size and length of fillets

LENGTH OF FILLET WELD →	1½"	2"	2½"			3"		
Ft. THICKNESS, THE THINNER MEMBER →	10G.	10G-3/16"	3/16-1/4"	1/4-5/16"	5/16-3/8"	3/8-1/2"	1/2-5/8"	5/8-3/4"
NOMINAL SIZE OF FILLET →	1/8"	1/8"+	3/16"	1/4"	1/4"	5/16"	3/8"	3/8"
SPACING, SHELL TO FLRS FORD FOR SEVERE SERVICE	6"	7"	9"	10"	10"	10"	10"	10"
" SHELL TO FLOORS ELSE WHERE	8(A)	9(A)	9"	10"	12"	12"	12"	12"
" SHELL TO FRAMES .125 OF LNTH FORD	7"	8"	9"	12"	12"	12"	12"	12"
" SHELL TO FRAMES ELSEWHERE	8"	9"	9"	10"	10"	10"	10"	12"
BRACKETS TO FRAMES, DECKS ETC DOUBLE CONTINUOUS								
SPACING, LONGITUDINALS TO SHELL	8"	10"	12"	11"	11"	12"	12"	12"
SPACING, SWASH BHDS			8"	9"	8"	9"	9"	8"
SPACING, NON-WATER TIGHT BHDS TO SHELL ETC		9"	9"	9"	9"	9"	9"	9"
SPACING ARND EDGES W.T.& OIL TITE BHDS CONTINUOUS 2 SIDES, ½ ft & OVER, CONT. 1 SIDE & INTERMIT OPP. SIDE ½ ft & UNDR (B)								
" STIFFENERS TO DEEP TANK BHDS			12"(A)	12"	11"	12"	12"	12"
" STIFFENERS TO ORDINARY BHDS & DK.HSE FRONT			12(A)	11"	11"	11"	11"	12"
" STIFFENER BRACKETS TO BEAMS, DKS ETC	DOUBLE CONTINUOUS							
" BEAMS TO DKS TO LONGIT BMS OR STRNGERS	9"	10"	12"	11"	11"	11"	12"	12"
" BEAM KNEES (BRACKETS) TO BEAMS & FRAMES DOUBLE CONTINUOUS								

A - FILLET WELDS TO BE STAGGERED, B - THE INTERMIT. WELDS TO BE SAME AS FOR DEEP TANK STIFNRS

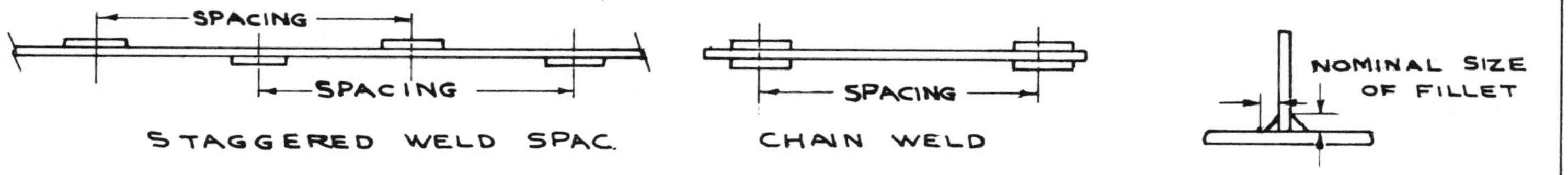

STAGGERED WELD SPAC.

CHAIN WELD

NOMINAL SIZE OF FILLET

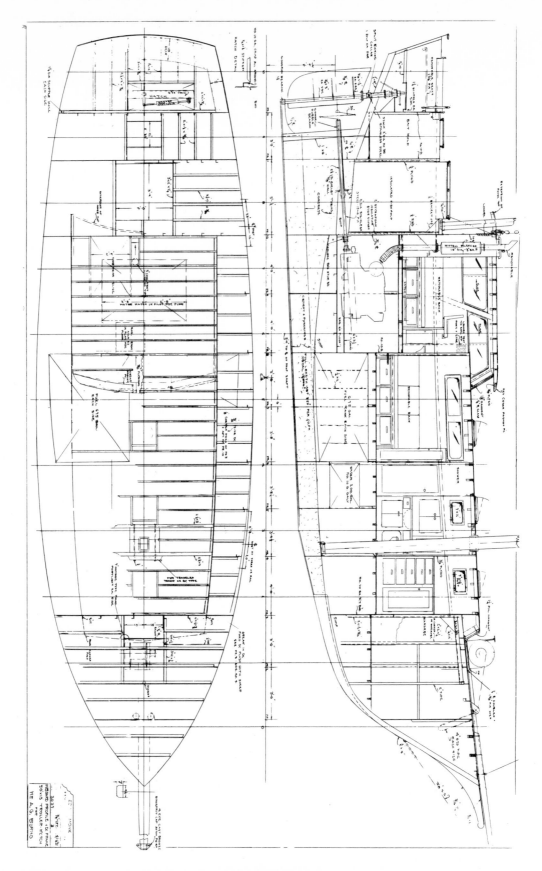

FIG. 129. Longitudinally framed, 50-foot ketch

whole plating can move with relative freedom. If, however, the horizontal seam is first welded, this will restrain the upper plates from moving when the butt is welded.

There are other recommended procedures, again written for a large hull with many plates constituting the shell.

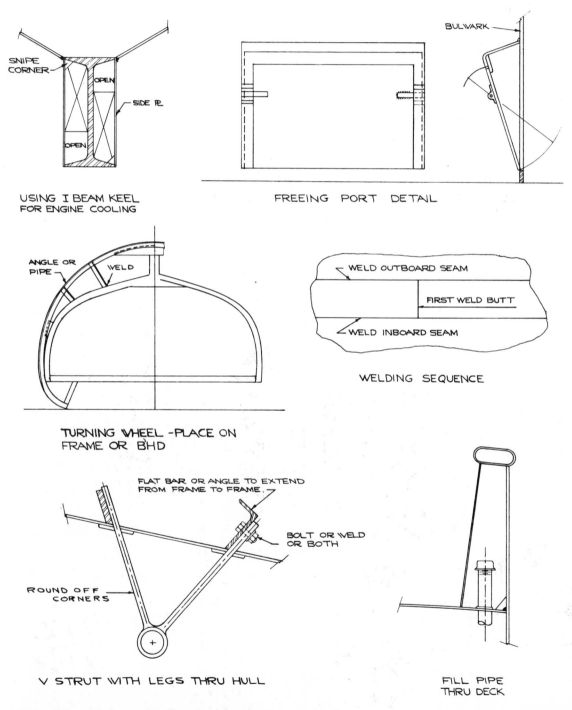

FIG. 130. Various details, steel boat

WORKMANSHIP

On butt welds a tolerance of ⅟₁₆″ plus or minus is permissible for the root opening in most joints.

General practice indicates a root opening of ⅛″ for ½″ plate and under. Root openings in excess of these amounts should be built up, and after build-up the edges should be dressed by grinding or chipping.

With ordinary mild steel of the thickness used on small vessels, no preheating is required except in cold weather, or about 32 degrees and colder. Rain and snow are not conducive to good welding. The additional quenching action of the rain and the water from melting snow increases the tendency to crack.

Some distortion is bound to occur and particularly so with the thinner plates used on small craft.

Two principal processes are used to straighten plate. One is line heating. This consists of applying heat close to the long sides of plates or panels or behind stiffeners and then quenching the heated spots with water spray. If further straightening is required, a second pass is applied a few inches from the first.

Spot heating consists of marking off the panel in squares of about six inches

FIG. 131. Dutch boat showing bilge keels and fin-type stabilizers

each and heating a spot about 1½″ diameter at the intersection of the lines to cherry red and cooling with water spray. The sequence is to start near the edges and work toward the center.

Another procedure is to cut a slot in the distorted part to relieve the tension and, after straightening by hammering, weld up again.

Almost all large paint manufacturers have their own schedule for treating steel. In all formulas, however, the metal is prime-coated almost immediately after removal of mill scale by sandblasting or other ways, as previously covered. The formulas, at least some of them, specify this, followed by one or two coats of zinc. The zinc must be protected by a barrier coat or coats. Above the waterline this is followed by color coats and below waterline by anti-fouling paint.

There are several problems peculiar to the welded metal hull caused generally by distortion. Struts are usually fabricated, welded up of flat bar for legs. No matter how carefully the strut is lined up it may be found out of line after welding in place. This also applies to shaft tubes. This is corrected in large shops by boring out the bearing hub or tube. One type of strut securement is shown in the illustration. This at least minimizes the distortion. A rubber bearing can accommodate a very small amount of misalignment. The bearing shell should not be brass, and most manufacturers can supply them with non-metallic shells.

Tanks, as previously mentioned, can advantageously be integral with the hull. On smaller boats the water tank should, however, be a separate tank, galvanized inside and out after welding—this because it is difficult to coat the inside of small integral tanks to prevent rusting.

Instead of the usual flush deck plate fill, the fill is often an extension of the fill pipe above deck, as per illustration. This is practical only if the filler pipe can be placed in an out of the way position such as inside the bulwarks. This type of fill pipe is more sanitary than the flush fill.

It is customary to concentrate all the through-hull connections for salt-water intake in one inlet called the "Sea Chest," generally in the engine compartment. This minimizes the danger of flooding through the failure of one of several intakes due to electrolysis and concentrates it in one spot where it can be watched. Also, the sea-chest pipe is generally specified of extra-heavy wall thickness, with particular care being taken in welding it to hull. If possible, it should be high or long enough to place the top above waterline so that its cap may be removed for inspection. It seems a prime choice for barnacle habitation, and of course it should be equipped with a screen at the hull, and the various spuds from it should each be valved.

Sea-water valves are a problem, for if of ferrous metal they will rust, and if of brass or bronze they are subject to electrolysis. Generally they are bronze, and the Society of Naval Architects recommends that a short length of heavier steel pipe be installed next to the valve. This is termed a "waste piece." It is expected to corrode, but, being heavier, it will last longer and should be so placed as to be easily replaced.

Common practice is to use copper or red brass pipe in small craft. Plastic (PVC) or fiberglass reinforced resin is of course not subject to corrosion and can be used where high temperatures are not involved. Use stainless-steel clamps.

Depth of well or height of solid bulwark in inches	Freeing port area in square inches per foot of bulwark length [1]
6	2
12	4
18	8
24	12
30	16
36	20

[1] Intermediate values of freeing port area can be obtained by interpolation.

FIG. 132. Freeing port table. Except as otherwise provided in this section, on vessels operating on exposed or partially protected waters, for each running foot of bulwark in the after two-thirds length of the vessel there shall be provided not less than the amount of freeing port area specified. The freeing ports shall be located so as to be effective considering probable list and trim. If the vessel is of such a design that there is not free drainage from the foredeck aft, then freeing ports shall be provided on the basis of the entire length of the bulwark fitted.

All seagoing boats should have freeing ports, and the U.S. Coast Guard specifies areas (Fig. 132). The first freeing port was hinged at top and tied at bottom with weak string or yarn that would break upon very slight pressure from inside. Shown here is a more sophisticated port that will not clang except under very severe circumstances.

Problems of the large ship, such as hull fractures, panting, and structural failures are rare in the relatively small craft with which we are concerned.

Electrolysis can be severe in the steel hull, as steel is the less noble metal to bronze in the electrolysis scale. Stainless-steel shafting should be used, and while stainless propellers are rather costly, they are available. Rudder stocks should also be stainless, and Number 316 is commonly used here. There are two or three stainless-steel shafts made expressly for propeller or tail shafting, and they should be used.

Bronze stuffing boxes are unavoidable, but they do not seem to give much trouble.

Several firms manufacture cathodic protection systems for metal boats, in which a small flow of electrical current counteracts the polarity of the natural action between the dissimilar metals.

FIG. 133. (Upper left) 67-foot, steel yacht-thwart ship framed at Amsterdam Shipyard Inc., Holland

FIG. 134. (Upper right) The same yacht with plating welded

FIG. 135. (Lower left) View of the yacht showing sprung teak deck, rails and stanchions, hatches and ventilators

FIG. 136. (Lower right) Trial trip

FIG. 137. Loading yacht aboard in Amsterdam, Holland

Most, or at least many, commercial operators depend on zinc anodes. These can be purchased with a welding strap cast in the zinc and are welded to the hull, generally a couple on each side of the keel and perhaps one on the rudder.

Should those not be available, a zinc plate should be bolted to the steel. A standard thickness for this purpose seems to be ⅝″, and a piece about 6″ wide and 12″ long is also common practice but smaller of course on rudders or other like places.

Material from *Ship Design and Construction,* pp. 276–77, 282–83, 268–69, by permission of The Society of Naval Architects and Marine Engineers.

15/ THE FERRO-CEMENT BOAT

THE LATEST THING IN BOAT BUILDING is ferro-cement. Actually the first boat of this material to gain prominence was built by Professor Nervi in Italy and launched in 1948. He is considered the father of the ferro-con boat. Shipwrecked sailors are credited with building a much earlier counterpart, at least using the same principle, of willow twigs and clay.

This is probably the most controversial of all building materials. There have been at least eight books written on the subject, and a list of several is given at the end of this chapter. They describe various methods of construction, starting with the original pipe frame.

FIG. 138. A ferro-cement troller and a ferro-cement ketch
Photo by Vincent Maggiora

In its favor is a low-cost hull, provided one can perform most of the work oneself. If it is built in a commercial shop using hired labor there would be little, if any, saving. It is of course impervious to the ship worm or to dry rot, is a fair insulator, and can take many hard knocks without damage. With the network of steel framing adequately protected from salt-water intrusion, electrolysis becomes a very small factor.

The thinnest practical shell is about ⅝″, and even with the use of lightweight aggregate it will weigh about 7.5 # per foot, or about the weight of 3/16″ steel. This is a handicap where a fast boat is concerned, but not so important on fishing boats, cruising sailboats, or for any boat use where speed or weight is not a major consideration.

There are about as many methods of construction as there are books on the subject. There are advantages to each.

The pipe method is perhaps the most simple, and a large number of boats have been built using it. Its chief disadvantage is sagging or distortion while cementing. Welding the cross-connections will remove most of this danger, though if high-tensile rod is used, the weld weakens the rod at the joining point and an unfair hull results.

At one time the cedar mold method was considered best. It faithfully preserves the shape, the rods can be stapled in place to the mold, and the hazard of sag is eliminated. It was found, however, that even with considerable use of a vibrator, penetration of the mix through the wire was difficult. The entire cedar planking of the mold has to be destroyed to get it out, leaving only the forms for a subsequent boat. Some recommend leaving the cedar planking in place for insulation and appearance. This, however, would seem to present some difficulty in attaching bulkheads, frames, etc. Should the builder, however, elect to use this method, I think ¾″ mesh poultry wire should be used for better penetration than can be had with hardware cloth. A gunite gun can successfully be used as the mold forms a backing.

With this construction, the builders of my acquaintance glue the bulkheads, engine stringers, etc., to the hull using epoxy glue, which forms a very strong bond. This, of course, is done after removal of the mold. Bulkheads may also be fiberglassed in place (see "The Fiberglass Boat"). Epoxy resin is used.

A third method is what might be termed the web frame, also referred to as the truss method, similar to a longitudinally framed metal boat where web frames and the bulkheads form transverse strength. This appeals to the writer as perhaps the most practical. It enables the builder to assemble the entire framework before cementing is started. Welding is necessary, so the advantage of high-tensile rods is largely lost.

Another *modus operandi* is the open mold as developed by John Sampson. Here you proceed as though you were building a bent frame wood hull (see Figs. 40 and 48) under the wood boat but lofted for all ribbands to be

FIG. 139. *Bobolink,* a 46-foot, ferro-cement troller-cruiser

FIG. 140.

(a) Cedar mold method—frame ready for planking

(b) Planked mold

(c) Applying the cement

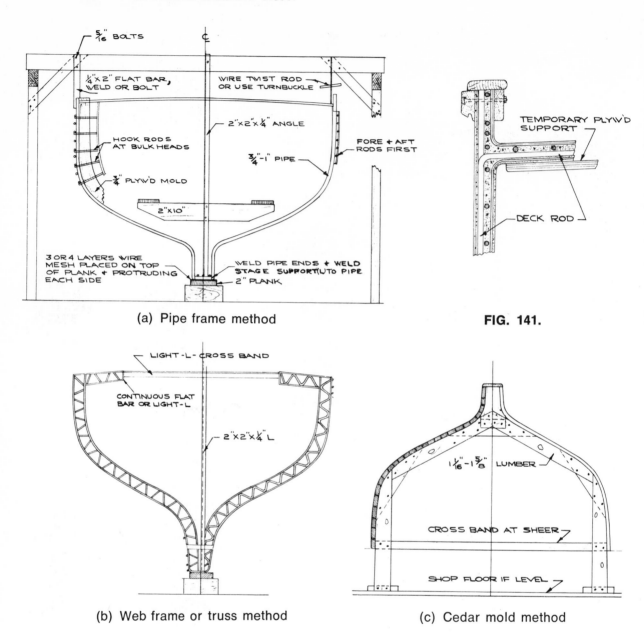

(a) Pipe frame method

FIG. 141.

(b) Web frame or truss method

(c) Cedar mold method

placed on the inside, so in lofting deduct for ribbands as well as hull thickness. Ribbands may be lighter than for bending oak frames, and 1⅝″ x 2½″ would be about right for a forty-footer if forms are spaced four feet or a bit less. Ribbands should be spaced closer at the bilge and wherever a tight bend occurs and should be almost clear to bend fair. They should be tapered at forward end as with a wood hull. The ribbands are spaced 8″ to 12″ centers. The high-tensile rods are best, as they will bend fair. The inner layers of mesh are first stapled on, followed

FIG. 142. Deck detail of *Bobolink*   *Photo by Vincent Maggiora*

by the rods, thwartship ones first, then the outer layers of mesh, using as small a staple as practical. Use as few as possible and keep away from the forms, for reasons that will be apparent later.

The open spaces between ribbands will enable the builder to wire the whole together, after which the ribbands are removed by sawing them off each side of the forms, using skil saw set to proper depth. Here you will see why the staples should be clear of forms. The short lengths at the forms can then be split out. Before this is done, drive large nails about four inches long, or No. 20D, into the forms adjacent to a longitudinal rod and one between each ribband. It will be advisable to drill for the nails. These are then welded to the longitudinal rods.

The hull may be set up either right side up or upside down. The latter would seem the most practical, provided means for turning over are available, and this should be done with the forms still in place.

FIG. 143. Interior of *Bobolink* looking aft   *Photo by Vincent Maggiora*

Plastering is no different from the pipe or web frame method. Adequate staging must be rigged to avoid standing on the frame. After the hull is cured the nails are burned off.

There are other framing layups, one in which the rods are run diagonally, the inside rods one way and the outer rods the other. This requires stout fore and aft members on top to counteract the bending moment at the top of the hull which is in effect a beam. As with all the several methods, three or four layers of mesh are applied inside the rods and the same number outside.

In all except the cedar mold method, the mesh must be laced or tied to the rods at about four-inch intervals, using No. 14–16-gauge soft wire. Some use one-half-inch hog rings and ring pliers, obtainable at upholstery supply houses.

Mesh can be one-half-inch or three-fourth-inch galvanized poultry wire or one-half-inch hardware cloth. The former is easier to apply. The entire hull surface must be fair, and a rubber hammer is used to help accomplish this.

With the pipe frame, hook rods, one-fourth-inch for boats up to about fifty feet, are placed to take the bulkheads and the web frames, if the latter are shown in the plan. A roughly fitting plywood form must be made at each one of these to obtain a straight frame or bulkhead. The hook rods are spaced about six-inch centers, one leg inserted between the mesh and lying parallel to the horizontal rods and the other against the plywood mold. Inside rod ends are trimmed off and a rod or ¼″ x 1″ flat bar is welded to them and the mold removed. The inside layers of mesh are worked around both sides and tied together as with the hull. Hook rods are also used for connecting deck to hull.

Assuming the builder is in possession of a set of plans adapted to one of the various construction methods, there are some things common with all of them.

Number 5 Portland cement is used, and to this is added Pozzolan, a bagged cementlike material that adds to the density of the finished product, making it more impervious to water absorption. Authorities differ on the amount to add, from 5 percent of the cement to 10 percent. I suggest the latter. Sand should be clean and sharp. Sand of granite or silica origin is excellent. Avoid sand of soft origin such as shale. Some builders substitute Saturnalite or other lightweight aggregate, accomplishing quite a saving in weight.

Mix one part of the Pozzolan-cement mixture to one part of sand by volume. Here again authorities differ, and one suggests one and three-fourths sand to one cement, which would seem a rather weak mixture. Use as little water as possible, as a stiff mix is less likely to slump. Use a paddle-type mixer and mix in small batches. You will soon see how large or small an amount is needed to keep up with the cementing crew.

All authorities recommend the builder employ professional plasterers or swimming-pool finishers, gathering together quite a crew, generally on a Saturday, for obvious reasons, and an attempt is made to complete the operation in one, perhaps long, work shift. Unless the cedar mold method is used, work from both sides.

Ending up with a fair hull is the most difficult part of it. The finisher will use a large trowel to attain this. A batten about ⅜″ x 1″, four feet long, grasped at each end and applied to the hull will disclose hollows and bumps.

It must always be kept in mind that you are dealing with a very heavy object, and the support for the hull must be adequate. A forty-six-foot finished hull will, for instance, weigh 15,000 lbs. or more.

Any of the various construction methods can produce a good boat, but the web frame seems, at least to me, the most promising, and it will be elaborated on here.

Lofting must of course be to the frames and bulkheads, after which one-fourth-inch plywood patterns are made, deducting for hull thickness, enabling the builder to transfer the shape to the assembly floor, which is covered with hard-surface one-half-inch asbestos board. Another line is drawn representing inside of frame or truss, and frames are used at each bulkhead. One-fourth-inch or larger rods, depending on size of boat, are bent to both these lines and held in place by nails or staples. A soft-type rod is used. Between these, short lengths are zigzagged as per illustration. The first half is removed and the second fabricated and then the two are joined together.

Assuming the boat will be set up right side up, the keel is always a problem if it is to provide support for the hull. William Roberts recommends removing the keel supports during construction, installing rods and wire in this area after the hull is so done, cementing the keel up perhaps six inches several days before the main hull, and replacing supports when cured.

The horizontal rods are placed first, welded to the web frames; transverse rods are seldom used; then the wire netting inside and out, and the inside layers

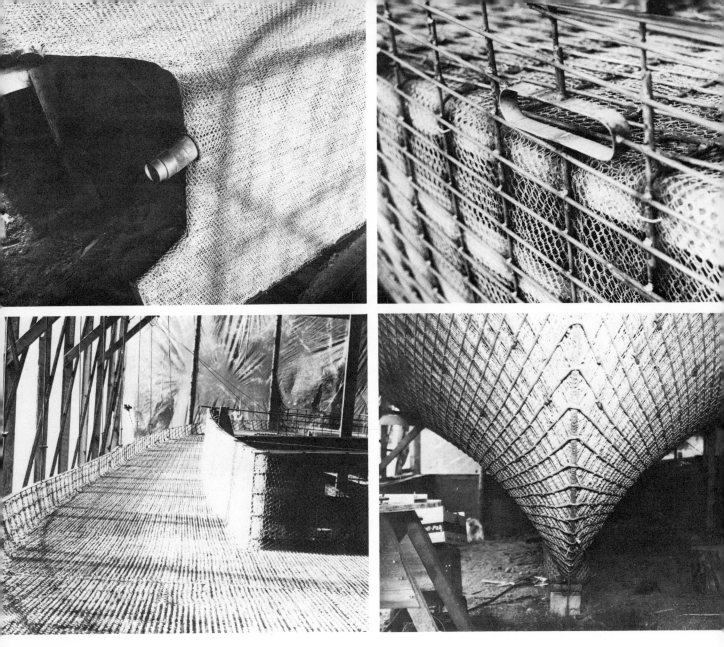

FIG. 144. (Upper left) Shaft tube and rudder and rudder port above it
Photo by Photocraft Studio

FIG. 145. (Upper right) Inside mesh in place and showing hook rods connecting
deck to hull. These photos are of a 48-foot cutter building by G. W. Stump,
Powell River, B. C.
Photo by Photocraft Studio

FIG. 146. (Lower left) Bow of 48-foot cutter
Photo by Photocraft Studio

FIG. 147. (Lower right) Deck of 48-foot cutter ready for cement
Photo by Photocraft Studio

are bent to cover the web frames. Plywood bulkheads will be bolted to some of the frames, so keep this frame face as smooth as possible.

Comes the deck: The longitudinal rods are laid first (some temporary shoring may be required), and after the netting is on, pieces of plywood must be wired to the underside, leaving about two inches at outboard side for cementing. Provided the plywood is not wired too tightly, the cement will penetrate under the longitudinal rods. Some use pegboard, which allows entrapped air to escape. Others dispense with any support and plaster the underside first and several days later, when this has hardened, the topside, first applying a cement wash.

Engine stringers and tank sides and ends can all be framed up, and the hull is ready for cementing.

Tanks can be built into a ferro-cement hull, though some commercial builders prefer to make at least the fuel tank separate and of metal, as with

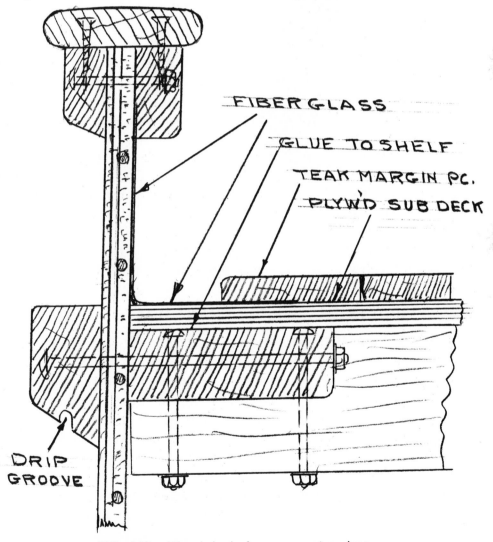

FIG. 148. Wood deck, ferro-cement cruiser

diesel the inside does not corrode and they can be made of mild steel at less cost than building them in.

The top is a problem with fuel tanks if built in, and this can be a slab of ferro-cement, fiberglassed plywood, or steel bolted or glued in place.

Fresh-water tanks are a natural, and often the top is of plywood. It can be epoxy-glued in place. Wood plugs must be inserted in cement for supply to galley, etc.

Wood decks are shippy, and can effect quite a saving in weight. The wood deck may be fiberglassed, but for beauty a teak deck laid in Thiokol is unsurpassed. It must, however, be laid over plywood for watertightness as shown.

Cabins are often of cement, and of course this solves any leak problem. However, it is heavy and its weight is high in the structure, whereas a wood house can present a finish inside, and portlights and glass are easily installed. The entire house exterior may be fiberglassed if desired.

In the web frame method the cement may be applied from inside, outside, or both sides at the same time, as your plasterer elects. The ideal temperature is 50 to 70 degrees. Between 40 and 50 degrees the water should be heated.

Portlight openings can be had by inserting a piece of three-fourths-inch plywood cut to shape. There are, however, tools that can cut out these holes later on, as well as holes for through-hull connections, etc., but the employment of these is generally expensive.

Curing the hull is important, and here again there is disagreement, the time it takes varying from seven to twenty-eight days. During the first part of this period the hull should be kept moist, either by spraying or covering with wet sacks, and it should be protected from the sun's rays. If the temperature is low, it should be draped with plastic sheet, carpet, etc., and an electric heater or two installed inside. Steam curing will shorten curing time to as little as twenty-four hours, but it involves more equipment and generally time is not that important.

PAINTING THE FERRO-CEMENT BOAT

When the hull is cured, it should be wire-brushed or rubbed with a coarse carborundum stone and etched with diluted muriatic acid. After this has been rinsed off it is given two coats of epoxy resin or other suitable coatings. This is important, as it forms a water barrier, protecting the vital steel work.

There are also other primers for ferro-cement boats manufactured by large paint firms that could very well effect a cost saving over the resin. Some state that this should not be done until ninety days have elapsed. At any rate it is best to postpone it as long as feasible.

After this the hull is painted in the usual manner with anti-fouling below the boot top and conventional marine paint above.

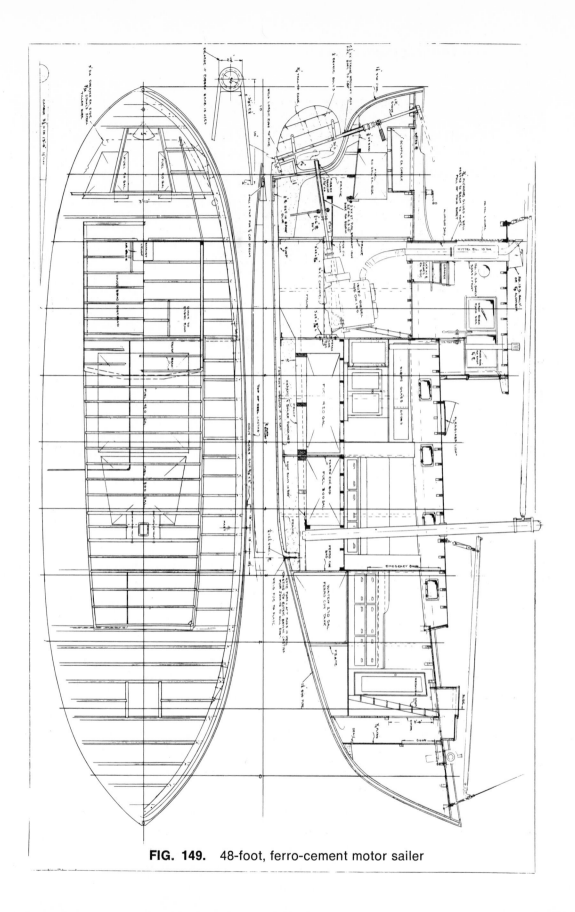

FIG. 149. 48-foot, ferro-cement motor sailer

FIG. 150. 47-foot, ferro-cement, off-shore cruiser—Captain Sam Guill, owner

SUMMARY

What has been written here is an attempt to cover each method of building to the point where the builder can construct his boat. However, each of these methods has been elaborated on in separate books, some including a history of ferro-cement and generally a number of designs which may be purchased from their author.

The open mold and the web frame are described in *Guide to Ferro-Cement* by William H. Roberts, Baycrete Marine, P.O. Box 57, Station B, Hamilton, Canada.

The pipe frame and cedar mold appear in *How to Build a Ferro-Cement Boat* by John Samson and Geoff Willens, Samson Marine Design Enterprises, Ltd., Ladner, B. C., Canada.

The pipe frame method is described in *Boat Building in Ferro-Cement* by Ross Harper, 5668 Kings Road, Vancouver, B. C., Canada.

Other books include *Boat Building with Hartley,* Box 30094, Takapuna North, Aukland, New Zealand; *Boat Building in Ferro-Cement* by Frank Carius N.A., 1471 Appin, N. Vancouver, B. C., Canada; and *Ferro-Cement Boatbuilding* by J. R. Benford, 1101 N. Northlake, Seattle, Washington.

16/ THE FIBERGLASS BOAT

FIBERGLASS BOAT PRODUCTION seems to have taken the boating industry by storm, though the advantages are most apparent only under quantity production.

There are many things going for it, including minimum of maintenance, weatherability, the fact that it does not shrink or swell, is not subject to the ship worm or to dry rot, is very strong, and can take a surprising amount of abuse.

FIG. 151. 34-foot, fiberglass fishing boat   *Photo by Bob Carver*

The major disadvantage is the fact that it is cold and the hull requires insulating if used in cold or cool weather. Some complain that the fiberglass hull is noisy. It may require painting after several years as the original finish becomes dull, although sanding with fine paper and then polishing will restore much of the original finish. Fiberglass resin will burn; however, there are fire-retardant resins available.

There seem to be two methods for the interior framing of the hull. Lloyds uses a series of half-round or top-hat stiffeners (see illustration), much as a round-bottom boat is framed, but spaced much farther apart.

The other method is to use four or more longitudinal bottom stringers, generally wood and fiberglassed to the hull. The stringers also serve as motor supports. Bulkheads and a few thwartship top-hat or half-round frames provide thwartship strength. Floor supports and other fore and aft members are also glassed in to provide added strength.

Lloyds' method is no doubt the lighter and uses less fiberglass, though most builders seem to prefer the other, as less labor is involved.

The decks, as well as superstructure, may be fiberglass, though this involves a mold and is not generally practical on a one-off boat. Instead, these are of plywood, fiberglass, or are teak-covered.

In all fiberglass work sharp corners are to be avoided, and at corners such as where deck meets house sides, there should be a cove. This can be done by use of fiberglass putty and running a round object along the corner to obtain a smooth fair shape.

Temperature is quite a factor. If too hot, the resin will set up too quickly, even setting up in the can before it can be used.

The cost of "one off," as it is termed, is generally high, though there are several procedures whereby it is not necessary to build a plug and mold, the most expensive part of the operation. These will be covered later.

In seeking the most authentic source, much of the following was influenced by *Glass Reinforced Plastic Boat Building,* written by Mr. A. McInnes and W. L. Hobbs for Lloyds Register of Shipping. Larry Belgrave of Holiday Boats, a pioneer in the industry, reviewed this chapter and added to it substantially.

The plug is the first step, and this consists of building a wood form the shape of the desired hull. Then a fiberglass shell is laminated over the exterior of the plug, which, when removed from the plug, becomes a mold, inside of which is formed the desired boat.

Some actually build a working wood hull, and after the mold has been taken off, it is finished as a boat. This, while dispensing with some wasted effort, involves considerable, though mostly recoverable, first cost.

The plug is built almost as though one were constructing a boat described under "The Wood Boat." The planking is usually cedar or pine about three-fourths inches thick or sometimes plywood for certain shapes. The molds or

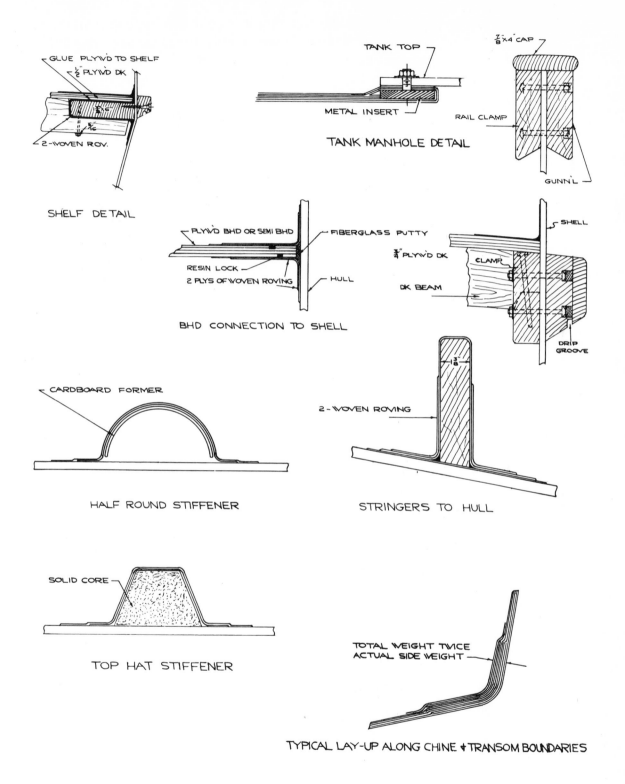

GLUE PLY'WD TO SHELF
½" PLY'WD DK
2-WOVEN ROV.

SHELF DETAIL

TANK TOP
METAL INSERT

TANK MANHOLE DETAIL

⅞"X4" CAP
RAIL CLAMP
GUNN'L

PLY'WD BHD OR SEMI BHD
RESIN LOCK
2 PLYS OF WOVEN ROVING
FIBERGLASS PUTTY
HULL

BHD CONNECTION TO SHELL

SHELL
¾" PLY'WD DK
CLAMP
DK BEAM
DRIP GROOVE

CARDBOARD FORMER

HALF ROUND STIFFENER

2-WOVEN ROVING
⅜

STRINGERS TO HULL

SOLID CORE

TOP HAT STIFFENER

TOTAL WEIGHT TWICE
ACTUAL SIDE WEIGHT

TYPICAL LAY-UP ALONG CHINE & TRANSOM BOUNDARIES

FIG. 152. Details, fiberglass boat

FIG. 153. Fiberglassing

(a) Applying the glass cloth

(b) Brushing in the resin

(c) Glassing in a bulkhead

(d) Hull interior showing laps in cloth

sawed frames are generally more closely spaced. The nail fastenings must be set and great care employed to obtain a smooth surface, as any imperfections will show in the fiberglass mold. Sometimes the plug is covered with glass cloth (or cloth with a thin mat laid under) and resin-coated for a better surface. This is followed by a 25-mil-thick colored gelcote which is sanded and buffed to a high polish.

The mold is next, and for separation of mold from plug one or two coats of mold release wax are then applied and polished. A parting agent, generally P.V.A. (poly-vinyl-acetate), is then sprayed lightly over the surface and allowed to dry. The mold gelcote, generally black, blue, or green in color, is sprayed on about 35-mm thickness and allowed to dry. The glass-mold lay-up is usually a thin mat (three-fourths- to one-and-one-half-ounce weight) covered by a six- to eight-ounce cloth as a first layer. Then alternate layers of one- to one-and-one-half-ounce mat and eighteen- to twenty-four-ounce roving or cloth are added (from two to four layers as required). When cured, it is quite limber and therefore must be supported by a framework of wood, plywood, or steel bars and pipes, which is glassed solid to the mold before removal from plug. This must be strong enough to hold the correct shape of the mold for all future usage and also must be able to support the extra weight of the boat formed inside of it. Should the boat have tumble home aft or other undercuts, a split mold (down the keel) may be necessary. On larger boats, the transom—or, on sailboats and some power boats, the keel—may be molded separately for quicker and easier work.

The finished, supported mold may be popped off by a combination of hoists and insertion of water and air between the mold and the plug, as well as some light rubber mallet tapping.

After removal from the plug, the mold usually requires smooth sanding and then polishing, which is the finishing touch to the mold. Next, to start the hull, again, the two coats of wax and buffing make it ready for the coat of P.V.A. and the gelcote (color of the boat). When this is dry, lamination, as described before but with the required plies of glass specified by the designer, forms the shell. With the easy availability of standard materials, it is wise to use the recommended materials rather than substitutes. P.V.A. and gelcotes can be applied with rollers, but the spraying method is preferred. A one-inch and a four-inch brush, a six-inch rubber squeegee, and metal-grooved or mohair, seven- to nine-inch rollers are used to spread the resin and to force it through the cloth, mat, and roving to evacuate the air and impregnate the glass material thoroughly.

Hull laminates should be thoroughly wetted with resin. No puddles or excess resin should be left on the surface or corners. A good laminate will have no white spots (too dry). All edges left to dry should be covered with finish mat strips for neater and easier covering. All edge cutting should be done at the semi-gelled stage when it is easy to cut with a sharp knife. In placing the material, seam edges should be arranged to double the keel or chine corners. All other edges should be lapped one to two inches. Shift laps two to six inches so that they do not come one over the other. The completed product must contain only enough resin to bond the glass fiber securely and to meet the U.S. Coast Guard specifications of 40 percent glass and 60 percent resin, approximately. Should the boat be subjected to Coast Guard inspection, one of the hull cutouts for through-hull fittings is submitted to them for analysis. It is burned in a laboratory and the remaining glass fibers weighed to determine the glass-fiber content.

Lloyds specifies that no more than eighteen hours elapse between laminate layers, but if more time has elapsed, the surface should be sanded. Also, wiping with a wet acetone rag softens the surface for a better bond. Lloyds also specifies that the hull be left in the mold at least twenty-four hours for curing and have a Barcol Hardness average of 40.

There are some sophisticated tools and methods used in laminating by boat shops. A wet-out gun is a great help at times. It shoots catalyzed resin right on the glass laminate, eliminating handling and mixing. A chopper-gun combination

FIG. 154. Thicknesses resulting from various laminates, 54-foot sport fisherman

Photo by Ray Krantz

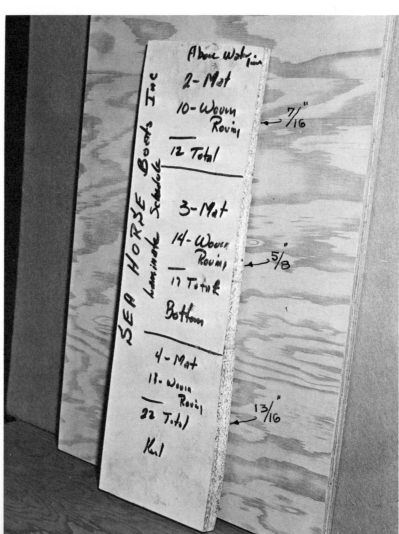

shoots catalyzed resin into a spray of chopped glass fibers about one to two inches long, which also saves cutting the pieces of mat to shape. The mat may be rolled down and a cloth or roving laid over it, with a little more resin applied to wet it out. There are some disadvantages to the chopper-gun, and hand lay-up, if done well, is generally conceded as resulting in a stronger hull.

Opinions vary as to laminates. Lloyds suggests alternating woven roving with mat. The technique in laying up is to apply a liberal coat of catalyzed resin first, lay the glass mat on it, and then apply more resin to wet out the mat. Then the cloth or roving is laid on the mat, adding enough resin to wet it. Roll and squeegee the roving and mat together to eliminate all air bubbles and dry spots, remove any excess resin, and cover edges with finish mat and resin.

Rollers can be purchased from the resin suppliers in various configurations. Those of metal or plastic with concentric rings will do a good job of rolling out the air bubbles and pressing the laminates together.

Building with a male mold requires that the hull thickness be deducted. The mold frames can be as light as three-fourths-inch thick, closely spaced, and the skin may be as light as one-fourth-inch plywood. The plywood is applied so

FIG. 155. Balsa-core, fiberglass hull ready for outer fiberglass skin

Photo by Ray Krantz

as to obtain a fair surface, and the edges should be fastened and glued to battens let in flush with the frames, much as with a plywood hull. This method requires more sanding to fair up the outside. The mold surface can be sanded smooth and sealed with a coat of shellac, varnish, lacquer, or even polyester resin. Then it must be waxed and a coat of P.V.A. applied for release. Gelcote, in this method, is put on last and must be of the air-drying variety for curing. The inside laminate would be put on first, usually roving and a mat about one-fourth-inch thick for the fifty-four-foot boat in the photo. The core, whether balsa wood, foam, or wood, would then be imbedded in resin as per supplier's recommendation. The outside layers of mat and roving, again about one-fourth inch for the fifty-four-footer, are then applied, finishing with cloth on the outside for a smooth surface. Lumps and bumps must be guarded against, and chine or keel corners must be faired as the lay-up progresses, to save unnecessary sanding. When using this method, all inside surfaces joining hull to bulkheads and stringers must be well sanded for good bonding. The photo shows a balsa core ready for the outside shell. After the outer shell has cured there will no doubt be some unevenness, and some builders apply one or two gel coats and sand this to obtain a smoother job.

There is some danger of the core separating from the shell from a hard impact; therefore care must be used to make sure the core is well bonded to the skin.

There are other core materials, one of them similar in appearance to styrofoam but harder and more resilient. It comes in sheets, and one advantage is that a lattice-type covering of light battens is placed over the forms. The sheets after heating are draped over the battens.

The outer fiberglass shell is applied and the whole turned over and the inside layers applied.

INDEX